Women of Might and Magic

Women of Might and Magic

Witch Queens, Deities of Death and Nature Goddesses in Finnish Mythology

Tiina Porthan

Illustrated by Tero Porthan

If you still don't obey,
I will find thy mother,
Who was born before the night,
I will fetch thy mighty parent.
Ancient Poems of the Finns

Contents

Introduction

Who are the goddesses of Finnish mythology? What are their powers and which realms do they govern? What do they look like?

Finland has a vast and intricate mythology. If you are not yet familiar with this tradition, this book opens up a whole new world for you.

In addition to the goddesses in the Kalevala, Finnish national epic, there are many other divinities who played a prominent part in the life of ancient Finns.

They appear in thousands of age-old poems, songs and spells that were passed on as oral tradition and later written down by collectors. Who are these women and how are they described in the poems?

From witch queens of the underworlds and nature goddesses of waters and forests, from goddesses of healing to goddesses of death, the female Finnish pantheon is one of a kind.

Part I: Queens of the North

Northland

Northland (Pohjola) is a mythical realm beyond nine forests and nine seas direction north or northeast at the edge of the world. It's a dark land with no Moon or Sun and so cold that the skin and shoes of the residents are on ice.

A traveller must overcome bears, wolves, fire pits and fiery eagles before arriving at the iron gates of this northern realm. Entrance is only possible for those with magical powers.

Pohjola is the birthplace of witches, diseases and beasts, and a place of death of the banished. It's ruled by witch goddess Louhi.

> *Thee I conjure away to murky Pohjola,*
> *To the doors of the gate of Pohjola,*
> *To the homes of the speckled lid,*
> *Where there is neither Moon nor Sun,*
> *Nor ever any day.*
> Magic Songs of the Finns

Louhi

Witch queen Louhi is the ruler of Pohjola and one of the protagonists of the Finnish epic, the Kalevala. With supreme magical powers of spellcasting, divination, summoning, conjuring, healing and metamorphosis, she rules Northland with a stern hand.

She's one of Death's daughters. Her realm is a land of death, a banishment place of murderers and evildoers and a land of decay where there is plenty of raw flesh, deer meat, bear bones, boneless meat and headless fish to eat and blood to drink.

An elk is hanging from a tree,
A noble reindeer has been killed,
A portly ox lies roasted there,
A great animal lies slaughtered there,
For a voracious man to eat,
For one a-hungered to devour.
Stags of the forest have been killed,
Beasts of the field been put to death,
There is boneless flesh to eat,
The blood of game to drink.
Magic Songs of the Finns

One of Louhi's greatest achievements is to invent the recipe for a magical device that will make her land into an affluent realm – at least for a while.

The word Louhi signifies a large rock or mountain. She governs the Iron Mountain of Northland, which in old Finnish cosmology is the center of the world. It supports the dome of the sky, and its top is attached to the North Star.

From the summit, one can descend nine fathoms deep to an underground cellar, a safe place for Louhi to hide her most valuable belongings. It's also a place of exile where witches banish one another to suffer for eternity. Another place of banishment is the maelstrom of the northern river, a whirlpool that swallows people, trees and whole ships into the deep.

> *Go now, where I command,*
> *Beyond nine seas,*
> *Beyond nine seas and a half,*
> *To the dark Northland,*
> *To the village of man-eaters,*
> *The village of drowners of heroes.*
> Ancient Poems of the Finns

Louhi is the mother and commander of many animals, diseases and natural phenomena like the wind, the frost and the fall of snow. She raises winds, conjures frosts, controls fire and even moves celestial bodies like the Sun and the Moon.

She's a seer with supernaturally precise senses. When sage Väinämöinen is lying close to death at the riverbank, she hears him all the way to her yard and knows it's an old man crying. She saves him by rowing him over the river to Northland and healing him.

Now she takes the hapless hero,
Lifts him from his bed of sorrow,
In her boat she safely seats him,
And begins at once her rowing,
Rows with steady hand and mighty
To her home upon the sea-shore,
To the dwellings of Pohyola.
There she feeds the starving hero,
Rests the ancient Wainamoinen,
Gives him warmth, and food, and shelter,
And the hero soon recovers.
Kalevala

With her divination techniques, she can predict whether war or peace is upon her realm. As a ship approaches Northland, she puts rowan branches in the fire. If they start trickling blood, the visitors are hostile, and if they trickle water, they come in peace.

In war, she conjures ships and armies with hundreds of swordsmen and thousands of archers and summons nature gods, diseases, bears and sea monsters against her enemies.

Louhi, hostess of Pohyola,
Called her many tribes together,
Gave the archers bows and arrows,
Gave her brave men spears and broadswords;
Fitted out her mightiest war-ship,
In the vessel placed her army,
With their swords a hundred heroes,

With their bows a thousand archers;
Quick erected masts and sail-yards,
On the masts her sails of linen
Hanging like the clouds of heaven,
Like the white-clouds in the ether.
Kalevala

Louhi is a master of metamorphosis who spies on her enemies in the form of a hawk and changes herself into a giant eagle-like creature that carries an army on her back.

Louhi, hostess of Pohyola,
Northland's old and toothless wizard,
Fastened wings upon her shoulders,
As an eagle, sailed the heavens,
Over field, and fen, and forest,
Over Pohya's many waters.
Kalevala

The Great Frost (Pakkanen), Louhi's son, is a powerful weapon of Northland whom she can send to freeze opponents. She gave birth to him among birch trees where he was rocked by the winds and breast-fed into full power by the snake goddess Syöjätär (Eateress).

Louhi sends him to the ocean to freeze Lemminkäinen's warship so he cannot reach Northland. Lemminkäinen utters all possible spells and manages to tame him, but since his ship is still frozen, he's forced to abandon it and continue on foot.

Louhi's Animals

Louhi's realm is protected by her animals. A fiery eagle keeps watch on the road to Northland, sharpening its beak and talons while waiting for travellers. The narrowest passageway is guarded by a wolf and a bear. Her yard is surrounded by an iron fence covered with snakes and the gate defended by a giant snake. Watchdogs around her mansion alert her at the slightest disturbance.

Louhi collects magical animals from other realms. Suitors who come to woo her daughter are given tasks to bring her legendary creatures, witch's assistants and animals of metamorphosis who can walk on mountains and glaciers or swim between realms.

The demonic Goblin's elk is famous for being impossible to catch, instead, it lures its hunters to the mountains of the otherworld where they get stuck inside snow. The Goblin's horse is a giant, fire-breathing horse with hooves of rock, legs of iron, back of steel and head of stone. It can go where others cannot, even climb the mountains of the underworld and carry witches and diseases on its back to their place of banishment.

Louhi is the forest goddess of northern forests. If hunters don't find game nearby, they ask her to open the gate to her forest and guide the animals with her palms across the river toward them.

> *Louhi, the mistress of Pohjola,*
> *Thrust forth thy woolly fist,*
> *Turn round thy hairy palm*
> *Before a man in search of game!*
> Magic Songs of the Finns

She's the mother of bears, wolves and lynxes. Bears are usually considered heavenly creatures born in the sky, but in an alternative birth myth, their mother is Louhi. She was walking along a

river in Northland when she felt her womb starting to ache. In great pain, she hid under a fir tree, gave birth to three hairy sons and named them Wolf, Lynx and Bear. They had no teeth and claws, but she made them from rowan and juniper roots.

She can summon bears from behind Northland's hills, and if a bear is seen near pastures, she's often suspected of having sent it to attack the cattle. In cattle-protecting spells, she's begged to chain her bears and hide their claws and teeth inside their fur so that they don't attack the cows or shepherds.

Louhi is the mother of dogs, and she controls their barking. To make a dog bark, she's asked to remove obstacles from its mouth, and to silence a dog, she will bind a silk band around its eyes, ears and nose so that it doesn't see, hear or smell a visitor.

Louhi, mistress of Pohjola,
Distinguished woman, Penitar,
From thy son remove impediments,
From the money-seeker, all obstacle;
Let the pup give tongue,
The dog bark openly,
Remove the stoppage from its nose,
The block across its scenting-horn.
Magic Songs of the Finns

She's also the mother of Musti, the iron-haired, fire-breathing dog that has iron teeth, a fiery throat, brass intestines and an iron heart. It's kept in chains in a castle and fed with butter, pork and eggs. The black dog is trained to bite and destroy enemy witches and eat their curses. Enemies are threatened with how the dog will eat them up until not a single bone is left.

Northern Witches

Northland is the home and birthplace of witches, and Louhi is their first mother. According to the origin myth, the witch was born behind Northland's hill on a dead tree bed on a pillow of stone.

> *Yes I know the birth of the witch,*
> *Where the witch was born,*
> *Behind the hill of Northland,*
> *On a bed of dead tree,*
> *On a pillow of stone.*
> Ancient Poems of the Finns

Witch parents usually teach their skills to a talented child. Louhi passes her wisdom on to her daughter, the Maiden of Northland, by teaching her divination techniques.

As a witch mother, she hosts sorcerers in her area and organizes spell meetings for them in her mansion that is so big that if a bird sings in the ceiling, its voice cannot be heard on the ground, and if a dog barks at the end of the hall, it cannot be heard at the door. During get-togethers, the benches are filled with witches, sorcerers, wizards and singers, and secret words are being muttered, spells being spoken and magic songs being sung.

The witches of Northland are age-old enemies of the sages of the land of Väinölä. Even before the world was born, a witch, who held an eternal grudge against sage Väinämöinen, shot him into the water with a poisoned arrow, which started the creation of the world. A diving duck laid an egg on his knee, and when he moved, the egg fell down and broke. Its lower part became the earth, the upper part the sky, the white part the Moon and the yellow part the Sun.

The Kalevala is built around the rivalry between Louhi and the sages Väinämöinen, Ilmarinen and Lemminkäinen. The mother of Lemminkäinen, a great sage herself, warns her son against going to Northland because the spells are strong and the witchcraft is different there.

"Do not go, my son beloved,
Ignorant of Pohya-witchcraft,
To the distant homes of Northland,
Till thou hast the art of magic,
Till thou hast some little wisdom,
Do not go to fields of battle,
To the fires of Northland's children,
To the slaughter-fields of Lapland,
Till of magic thou art master."
Kalevala

Northland is the home of diseases but also healers, and northern witches have healing expertise not found elsewhere. They are specialized in healing burns, boils, bleedings and frostbite.

In the oldest poem where Louhi appears with that name, she appears as a healer of damages caused by fire. She's pleaded to travel from the north wearing her iron gloves, grab the fire and place a water lily around the patient's hands to heal the burns.

Louhi, Hostess of Northland,
Bring your iron gloves,
Bring your copper mittens,
With which to grab the fire,
Put the whole hand to the flames,

Louhi, Hostess of Northland,
Place a water lily,
On two sides of my palm,
That fire has burnt,
That the flames have stolen.
Ancient Poems of the Finns

In another spell, read in a healing ritual in the sauna, Louhi is asked, together with nature's daughters, to draw the disease away from the patient. The disease is told to take the Goblin's horse and ride up north, through the gates of Northland and over the Iron Mountain into the whirlpool of the northern sea.

Northern healers swallow fire to appease its wrath, drink blood from wounds, use a plug to stop bleedings and crush boils with eagle's claws.

An old wife lives in Pohjola
Who can inform how a tumor should be squeezed,
An evil swelling should be pressed
With an eagle's powerful claws,
With the talons of the bird of air,
With which I shall the tumors claw,
Shall also press the swellings down.
Magic Songs of the Finns

Sampo, the Magic Mill

Louhi wants to transform her land into an affluent realm and starts designing a device that could fulfill her dream.

She creates a recipe for Sampo, a magic mill. The ingredients needed are a tip of a swan's feather, lamb wool, a barren cow's milk and a grain of barley.

> *Thus replied the hostess, Louhi:*
> *"Him alone I'll give my daughter,*
> *Promise him my child in marriage,*
> *Who for me will forge the Sampo,*
> *Hammer me the lid in colors,*
> *From the tips of white-swan feathers,*
> *From the milk of greatest virtue,*
> *From a single grain of barley,*
> *From the finest wool of lambkins."*
> Kalevala

Someone is needed to forge the mill. Louhi promises Väinämöinen that she will let him leave Northland if he sends over a blacksmith skilled enough to forge the Sampo. There's only one person who can perform the task. Blacksmith Ilmarinen, the discoverer of iron, has forged the sky dome with stars so skilfully that no hammer traces or tong marks are to be seen. Väinämöinen sends him to Northland.

Ilmarinen sets up a smithy at the Iron Mountain and starts working day and night, using the ingredients given by Louhi. On the first day, a bow emerges from the forge, on the second day a boat, on the third day a cow and on the fourth a plough.

Frustrated, Ilmarinen summons the winds to help him. The east wind rushes, the west wind roars, the south wind cries and the north wind howls, and at the end of that day, the Sampo rises from the fire, its lid sparkling with stars like the dome of the sky.

The Sampo starts grinding, offering all good things and riches: flour, money, salt, things to eat, things to sell and things to keep. Louhi hides the mill inside the Iron Mountain behind nine locks and roots it deep in the earth. The land of death has become a wealthy realm.

> *Joyfully the dame of Northland,*
> *Louhi, hostess of Pohyola,*
> *Takes away the magic Sampo,*
> *To the hills of Sariola,*
> *To the copper-bearing mountains,*
> *Puts nine locks upon the wonder,*
> *Makes three strong roots creep around it;*
> *In the earth they grow nine fathoms,*
> *One large root beneath the mountain,*
> *One beneath the sandy sea-bed,*
> *One beneath the mountain-dwelling.*
> Kalevala

Louhi's Metamorphosis

The wizards start wondering why Northland has become so powerful when in fact it was them who forged the Sampo, and it should belong to them. They sail to Northland to negotiate with Louhi about sharing the mill, but when she refutes their suggestion, they decide to steal it. They put everyone to sleep, pull the Sampo out of the mountain with a giant ox and start the journey back.

When waking up, Louhi is so infuriated by the theft that she summons thunder god Ukko to raise a storm, the Mist Maiden to create a fog and sea monster Iku-Turso to stop their ship from advancing.

"Iku-Turso, son of Old-age,
Raise thy head above the billows,
And destroy Wainola's heroes,
Sink them to thy deep sea-castles,
There devour them at thy pleasure,
Bring thou back the golden Sampo,
To the people of Pohyola!"
Kalevala

Väinämöinen fights back all the obstacles. Louhi calls her tribes together and conjures a warship with an army to go after them, but a reef conjured by Väinämöinen breaks the ship and its pieces fall into the sea.

Enraged, Louhi makes her most impressive metamorphosis yet by transforming herself into a giant eagle-like warbird that carries a hundred swordsmen under her wing and a thousand bowmen on her tail.

Quick she changes form and feature,
Makes herself another body;
Takes five sharpened scythes of iron,
Also takes five goodly sickles,
Shapes them into eagle-talons;
Takes the body of the vessel,
Makes the frame-work of an eagle;
Takes the vessel's ribs and flooring
Makes them into wings and breastplate;
For the tail she shapes the rudder;
In the wings she plants a thousand
Seniors with their bows and arrows;
Sets a thousand magic heroes
In the body, armed with broadswords
In the tail a hundred archers,
With their deadly spears and cross-bows.
Kalevala

She reaches the thieves' ship and tries to take the Sampo, but Väinämöinen hits her talons with an oar so that the mill falls into the sea. Louhi tries to grab it with one finger but only manages to save the lid. The Sampo breaks into pieces that are scattered in the ocean, and its loss brings poverty to Northland.

Louhi's Revenge

Louhi is not finished with the ones who brought misery to her land. After all, the Sampo was her invention, and she commissioned its creation. She decides to take revenge against the ones who took it from her.

First, she sends nine deadly diseases – Colic, Pleurisy, Fever, Ulcer, Plague, Consumption, Gout, Sterility and Cancer – to attack the people of Väinölä.

Louhi, hostess of Pohyola,
Banished all the other children
To the fog-point in the ocean,
To the island forest-covered;
Banished all the fatal creatures,
Gave these wicked sons of evil
To the people of Wainola,
To the youth of Kalevala,
For the Kalew-tribe's destruction.
Quick Wainola's maidens sicken,
Young and aged, men and heroes,
With the worst of all diseases,
With diseases new and nameless;
Sick and dying is Wainola.
Kalevala

Väinämöinen fights back the diseases and heals his people. Next, Louhi raises the mighty bear of Northland against Väinölä's cattle.

Louhi, hostess of the Northland,
Toothless dame of Sariola,
Envy-laden, spake these measures:
"Know I other means of trouble,
I have many more resources;
I will drive the bear before me,
From the heather and the mountain,
Drive him from the fen and forest,
Drive great Otso from the glen-wood
On the cattle of Wainola,
On the flocks of Kalevala."
Thereupon the Northland hostess,
Drove the hungry bear of Pohya,
From his cavern to the meadows,
To Wainola's plains and pastures.
Kalevala

Väinämöinen performs a hunting ritual that ends with a bear feast. When Louhi hears the sounds of the celebration and sees the Sun and the Moon shine their light on Väinölä, she grabs the celestial bodies and hides them inside the Iron Mountain. She also steals the fire from them to make their mansions cold and dark.

Louhi, hostess of Pohyola,
Northland's old and toothless wizard,
Makes the Sun and Moon her captives;
In her arms she takes fair Luna

From her cradle in the birch-tree,
Calls the Sun down from his station,
From the fir-tree's bending branches,
Carries them to upper Northland,
To the darksome Sariola;
Hides the Moon, no more to glimmer,
In a rock of many colors;
Hides the Sun, to shine no longer,
In the iron-banded mountain.
Kalevala

Väinämöinen finds the Sun and the Moon inside the mountain but can't open the locks, so he returns to blacksmith Ilmarinen for keys. Transforming herself into a hawk, Louhi flies to spy on them and sees Ilmarinen forging a collar they will use to bind her inside the Iron Mountain for good.

She flies back to Northland, opens the locks and returns in the form of a dove to tell the blacksmith that the Sun and the Moon have been released.

The story of Sampo is part of the world's creation myth, recited during sowing and fishing seasons. It explains the origin of agriculture because when it broke, its pieces became grains and riches of the sea.

Maiden of Northland

Louhi's daughter, the Maiden of Northland (Pohjan neiti), is famous for her beauty. From her temples beams the moonlight, from her breast the sunshine, from her forehead the rainbow and from her neck the seven stars of the Great Bear.

Like the goddesses of the Sun and the Moon, she sits on a rainbow weaving golden and silver fabrics with a golden spindle. She's famed across the land and finest of the waters. All of Northland sings her praises, but she's known for not accepting a husband.

In the Northland lives a virgin,
In a village there, a maiden,
That will not accept a lover,
That a hero's hand refuses,
That a wizard's heart disdaineth;
All of Northland sings her praises,
Sings her worth and magic beauty,
Fairest maiden of Pohyola,
Daughter of the earth and ocean.
From her temples beams the moonlight,
From her breast, the gleam of sunshine,

From her forehead shines the rainbow,
On her neck, the seven starlets,
And the Great Bear from her shoulder.
Kalevala

She has conversations with birds, asking them for advice regarding matters of the heart. One day, she asked a robin which would bring more happiness, living at home with her parents or as a daughter-in-law in her husband's house. The bird told her that life in her parents' house is like a day in the sun, whereas the life of a daughter-in-law means living like a dog in chains.

The maiden has magical powers but is not yet as powerful as her mother. Louhi teaches her divination methods by showing her how rowan branches put in fire will show whether a friend or foe is approaching. If they trickle honey, it means a suitor is on his way.

Northland's fair and slender maiden,
Beautiful and modest daughter,
Lays a sorb-branch on the fire-place,
Lights it with the fire of magic;
Does not trickle drops of scarlet,
Trickles neither blood, nor water,
From the wand come drops of honey.
Kalevala

Sage Väinämöinen arrives and suggests marriage, and the maiden starts giving him impossible tasks like splitting a hair with a tipless knife, peeling bark from a stone and pulling an egg into a knot. He performs the tasks, but then the maiden sends him to build a boat from the splinters of her spindle and the fragments of her distaff and push it to the water without his knee, arm, hand or foot touching it. He starts building the boat but is injured because the Hiisi goblin pushes his axe causing a bleeding wound.

Meanwhile, another suitor arrives. Louhi has earlier promised her daughter to blacksmith Ilmarinen in exchange for the Sampo. But even if he forged the mill, the girl doesn't want to leave with him, explaining that she cannot leave the birds because no-one else can make them sing but her.

A third suitor, wizard Lemminkäinen arrives. Louhi gives him a task to shoot the swan of Tuonela with one try and one arrow. This is practically a death sentence because even an attempt to kill this sacred bird will be punished by the dead. Lemminkäinen dies performing this task.

Blacksmith Ilmarinen hasn't given up. He returns, and Louhi gives him a task of ploughing a field of serpents and bringing her the bear, wolf and pike of Tuonela. The maiden, who has now taken interest in Ilmarinen, gives him advice on how to succeed.

For the field, he should forge a plough of gold and silver, for the bear and wolf a bridle of steel and halter of iron, and to catch the pike, he must make an iron eagle. Ilmarinen succeeds in all the tasks. They have a wedding celebration and move to live together.

After a while, Kullervo comes to their household to work as a slave. He's a troubled character with magical powers whom his previous family tried to drown, burn and hang.

The maiden sends him to work as a shepherd and bakes a stone inside his snack bread. When Kullervo cuts into the bread, he breaks his father's knife and gets mad at her.

He summons bears and wolves to the pasture, turns them into cows and brings them back to the barn. When the maiden starts milking them, they change back into their true form and attack her, tearing her face and breaking her legs. At the last minute, she tries to summon thunder god Ukko to save her, but it's in vain, and she dies.

Ice Girl

The Ice Girl (*jäinen neiti*) is a goddess of ice who lives in an icy well in a frosty spring in Northland. Her skin is icy, her socks, shoes and mittens are on ice, and ice lumps hang from the hem of her frozen, snow-covered dress.

> *A frosty maiden, an icy girl,*
> *Sits in a crouching attitude*
> *At the mouth of a frosty spring,*
> *In the hollow of an icy well,*
> *A golden ladle is in her hand,*
> *With which she draws the water up.*
> Magic Songs of the Finns

When the first fire was struck in the sky, it fled down to earth, and the Ice Girl was called to help. With a golden ladle, she took icy water and slush from the spring and put them into kettles on a sledge.

Carrying one hunk of ice on her bosom and one under her arm, she pulled the sledge through the snow castle of Northland, out the gates, over nine seas and through eight villages.

Upon arrival, she threw ice and icy water on the damages caused by fire. It appeased the fire's wrath and removed the pains. She was assisted by a bee who flew with six cups of healing ointments on its back and sprinkled them on the burns.

> *Rise, maiden, from the dell,*
> *From the moist earth,*
> *Dear lass from inside a frosty spring,*
> *From the hollow of an icy well,*
> *Thy shoes and laces all over ice,*
> *The folds of thy skirt all over rime,*
> *Thy jacket a mass of ice,*
> *Thy clothes entirely hid with snow,*
> *In thy bosom a hunk of ice,*
> *Under thine arm a lump of ice.*
> Magic Songs of the Finns

The Ice Maiden can be summoned with spells to travel from Northland whenever there is fire and bring with her ice and snow.

> *O frosty maiden, the icy girl,*
> *When needed, hither come,*
> *Bring snow for sores made by Fire,*
> *For the injuries by Panu frost,*
> *Snow-lumps from the bed of a lamb,*
> *Some ice from the pen of a full-grown sheep,*
> *With these snow-lumps form a crust,*

With the ice form a coat of ice
With which the seas are crusted o'er,
The lakes are coated o'er with ice.
Magic Songs of the Finns

Loviatar

Loviatar, Louhi's incarnation, is the mother and goddess of diseases, whose name variations include Loveatar Nature's Wife, Louhiatar Old Wife, Lokahatar Sturdy Wife and Lohetar Beautiful Wife.

Her story – the origin myth of diseases – is told during healing rituals because healers need to name the disease, its birthplace and its mother in order to take it under control and cure the patient. The myth explains the stages of Loviatar's impregnation and childbirth in great detail.

Loviatar was walking on a road in Northland and decided to lie down in the middle of the road with her back to the wind. The north wind started blowing, raised her skirt and impregnated her.

> *The powerful woman Louhiatar,*
> *Pohja's ragged-tailed old wife,*
> *That has a swarthy countenance,*
> *A skin of hideous hue,*
> *Was walking along a path,*
> *Was creeping along the course;*
> *On the path she made her bed,*
> *On the course her sleeping-place,*
> *She lay with her back to the wind,*

With her stern to a chilly blast,
With her groin to a fearful storm,
With her side due north.
There came a great gust of wind,
From the east a tremendous blast,
The wind raised the skirts of her furs,
The blast the skirts of her petticoat,
The wind got the dolt with child,
It quickened her into pregnancy
On an abandoned naked field,
On a tract without a knoll.
Magic Songs of the Finns

Her pregnancy was long and painful and lasted for nine months, three years, nine years or even sixty years.

Thus she carried a heavy womb,
A bellyful of suffering;
Two summers she carried it,
She carried it two, she carried it three
Seven summers she carried it,
Eight years at any rate,
Nine years in all, less by nine nights.
Magic Songs of the Finns

When the time of childbirth grew near, in great agony, she tried to give birth under a rock, on a water lily in a pond, inside an iron barrel, in the surge of a fiery river, on sauna stones and on the top of the Iron Mountain.

She tried to reduce her wame,
To lighten by a half her womb,
In the space between two rocks,
In the nook between three boulder stones,
Inside the walls of a fiery stove,
In a stove of stone,
In a barrel of oak,
Within iron hoops,
At the brink of fiery rapids,
In the eddy of an awful stream.
In these her belly was not reduced,
No lighter became the wretch's womb.
The foul creature began to weep,
To shriek, to bewail herself,
She knew not whither she should go,
In what direction she should move
To relieve her wame,
To bring to birth her progeny.
Magic Songs of the Finns

The delivery finally succeeded on a rock in the river and lasted for three years. She gave birth to nine boys and named them diseases: Boil, Stitch, Tooth Worm, Rickets, Colic, Plague, Scab, Gout and Ague. The names vary from poem to poem, but all in all, she has given birth to countless diseases, including abscess, pox, fever, rigors, fits, pains, cancer and sudden death.

> *She squeezed up one into a boil,*
> *She stiffened another into scab,*
> *She pricked one into pleurisy,*
> *She formed another into gout,*
> *By force she made one into gripes,*
> *She chased another into fits,*
> *She crumpled one into sudden death,*
> *Into rickets she cut up another one.*
> Magic Songs of the Finns

Loviatar sent her sons to the world. To Stitch, she gave arrows to shoot into people, and to Gout, a plane to cause joint pain. The diseases can be commanded by those with magical powers. Witches throw Boil or Scab against a person's skin, send Colic to gnaw on their intestines and Tooth Worm into their mouth to eat their jaws and teeth.

> *Tore one into being Atrophy,*
> *She designated one the Worm,*
> *Struck one into being a Cancerous Sore,*
> *Made one an Eater of the Heart,*
> *Another to eat up furtively,*
> *One to stab openly,*

To claw the limbs with violence,
To cause an aching in the joints.
One she formed into Gout,
And into his hands put a plane,
Pricked one into being Pleurisy,
And arrows she put in his fist,
In his wicker basket spears.
Magic Songs of the Finns

Healers banish the diseases back to Northland, their birthplace. The disease is threatened that if it doesn't agree to leave, the healer will go and find its mother Loviatar and tell her about its evil deeds.

I will banish thee still farther,
To the Northland's distant borders,
To the broad expanse of Lapland,
To the ever-lifeless deserts,
Go, thou monster, hence to wander,
Flee this place, thou plague of Northland,
Ere I go to seek thy mother,
Tell the ancient dame thy mischief;
She shall bear thine evil conduct,
Great the burden she shall carry;
Great a mother's pain and anguish,
When her child runs wild and lawless.
Kalevala

Nameless Daughter

After giving birth to nine boys that became diseases, Loviatar gave birth yet to another child, a girl.

She brought nine sons to birth,
The tenth was a female child,
On a single summer night,
From a single filling of the womb.
Magic Songs of the Finns

She could not find a name for her, so she sent her to the river to become a sorceress and fill the world with witches. In the Kalevala version, Loviatar only has nine children, all of them boys, and the tenth girl is not mentioned.

Thus she ordered her away,
To the rough Rutja rapids,
To the fiery foaming surge,
From her were bred the frosts,
From her were born the Syöjätärs,

From her other calamities,
Wizards to the waters,
Witches to every creek,
Envious to every place,
In the rough Rutja rapids,
In the fiery foaming surge.
Ancient Poems of the Finns

Sent away by her mother, alone on the sea, the nameless girl gave birth to witches, wizards, the envious and the water goddess Syöjätär (Eateress) who in turn brought snakes, lizards and trees to the world.

To one she could not find a name,
So she ordered her
To the harsh stream of Rutja,
From her, Syöjätär was born.
Ancient Poems of the Finns

It's unknown how she gave birth, but Luonnotars, nature goddesses, usually create animals and other beings from their hair, saliva or tears by spitting in the water, shaking off a hair or letting a tear fall.

The pine grew from a strand of hair that fell when a Luonnotar was running over swamps, lands and fields shaking off some of her hair, and the birch from a tear that fell down her cheek to her feet.

They also create by rubbing their palms together, by milking from their breasts or by dropping pearls and pins to the ground. Lizards were born from a pearl that fell from a Luonnotar's bosom when she was stepping from stone to stone, and vipers were made by her spinning an iron thread in a spinning wheel. Like Loviatar, they can also be impregnated by the winds.

A maid was sitting on a stone,
On a rock a woman had set herself,
She is brushing her hair,
Is arranging her head.
One of the maiden's hairs fell down,
One of the woman's hairs broke off,
A wind then carried it away
To a meadow without a name;
From that a wasp was made,
An evil bird was caused to dash
With a copper quiver on its back;
Its quiver is full of poisoned stings.
Magic Songs of the Finns

Syöjätär

Syöjätär (Eateress) is a nature goddess born in deep water from Loviatar's nameless daughter whom her mother tossed into the river. She's the mother of snakes, the foster mother of stones, wet nurse of the frost and an earth goddess linked to sowing and the birth of trees.

> *Syöjätär was born in the deeps,*
> *On the smooth waves,*
> *On the clear open seas.*
> Ancient Poems of the Finns

She can be seen sitting on a rock brushing her hair or rowing a boat with a red sail. Nicknamed fire-throat, she has a mouth in the middle of her head and a tongue in the middle of her throat. She has eaten hundreds of men and destroyed thousands of full-grown men.

> *Syöjätär on a lake was rowing,*
> *The fiery throat was bobbing*
> *In a copper boat with scarlet sail.*
> *There is the Syöjätär in the sea,*
> *With a mouth in the middle of her head,*

A tongue in the middle of her throat,
Who has eaten a hundred men,
Destroyed a thousand full-grown men.
Magic Songs of the Finns

She can be summoned from the sea to fight against one's enemy. Healers call her to help in removing witch's arrows from a patient. When the first arrows were shot, she rose from the sea breaking a boat's iron hull to collect the arrows in her lap. Whoever shoots arrows into people or animals is threatened with Syöjätär. She has jaws like six axe handles and she will rise from the sea and eat the shooter.

Rise, Syöjätär, from the sea,
Through a boat's iron hull,
Through a barque of iron,
Rise, Syöjätär, from the sea,
With a mouth in the middle of the head,
With jaws like six axe handles,
She has eaten a hundred men,
Destroyed a thousand males,
May she eat you too!
Ancient Poems of the Finns

Syöjätär is the mother of snakes. She gave birth to them by spitting in the water. Her spit was rocked by water gods, lengthened by the winds, softened by the Sun, made shiny by the Moon and carried to the shore by the waves. It took anywhere from seven summers to seven hundred years.

Syöjätär once let her spittle,
Fall upon the waves of ocean;
This was rocked by winds and waters,
Shaken by the ocean-currents,
Six years rocked upon the billows,
Rocked in water seven summers,
On the blue-back of the ocean,
On the billows high as heaven;
Lengthwise did the billows draw it,
And the sunshine gave it softness,
To the shore the billows washed it,
On the coast the waters left it.
Kalevala

On the shore, beings from the underworld gathered to mold the snake into its final form. Its back was made of the fire poker of the Hiisi Queen, eyes of the seeds of Lempo, snout of Tuoni's sprout, mouth of Syöjätär's clasp, teeth of the Hiisi girl's needles, gums of Kalma's maiden's gums and heart of the heart's core of its mother.

From what was the mouth prepared?
From the clasp of Syöjätär.
From what was thrown the heart?
From the heart's core of Syöjätär.
Magic Songs of the Finns

Snakes are called Syöjätär's buckle jewels, and she continues to be responsible for their deeds. If a snake bites, healers threaten it with searching Syöjätär from the bottom of the sea and telling her about its evil acts so that she can discipline them.

Also wolves and lizards originate from her spit. Lizards were born from nature goddess Kasaritar who became pregnant after eating her spit, and wolves from Kuolatar, Lady of Saliva, who rose from her spit and rubbed some fluff between her palms.

Syöjätär is linked to the earth, stones and trees. She has sown lands and swamps to grow heather, pines and willows and created the fir tree with other earth goddesses.

> *Syöjätär was sowing the hills,*
> *Sowing the swamps,*
> *Heather was growing,*
> *Sowing the hills,*
> *Pines were growing,*
> *Sowing the dells,*
> *Willows were growing.*
> Ancient Poems of the Finns

Syöjätär is the foster mother or wet nurse of different beings. Stones, Syöjätär's sweethearts, are grown inside the earth and lulled in a golden cradle by earth goddesses. She has breast-fed the Great Frost, Louhi's son, into a powerful being.

> *Pakkanen, Great Frost,*
> *Son of Puhuri,*
> *How did you grow so cold,*
> *How did you get so strong?*

Syöjätär breast-fed you,
With nipples without tips,
With breasts without heads.
Ancient Poems of the Finns

Witches and the Envious

Loviatar sent her daughter to the world to populate every lake with witches, every door with sorcerers, every fence with diviners, every path with sootsayers and every place with the envious.

Wizards there are in every dell,
And sorcerers at every gate,
Diviners are at every fence,
Soothsayers are on every path.
Magic Songs of the Finns

Witches were born behind Northland's hill when snakes were crying. Witches stemming from Northland are more powerful than other sorcerers. They're even stronger if they were born from a witch parent who teaches them magic and performs an initiation ritual by washing their child at a river before it's three days old. Louhi has taught her daughter divination.

Various divination tools like a sieve are used to gain information about, for example, where a lost animal is, how an endeavour will succeed, who the thief is, who has caused an accident or where a disease came from.

Charms are used to tame forces like fires or bears and invert events, for instance, by making a thief return stolen goods. Protection spells are used to ensure the success of livelihoods like the preparation of milk and butter. Magical protection gear is conjured when taking on difficult tasks like expelling diseases. Strong witches can summon nature gods and goddesses to help them.

> *May I be clothed with a burning coat,*
> *With furs of fiery red,*
> *That Hiisi's folk may be confused,*
> *Earth's awful beings may be abashed*
> *While this sorcerer uses magic arts.*
> Magic Songs of the Finns

The envious (*kade*) are witches who act out of envy, causing nuisances to other people's family and livelihood. They spy and eavesdrop behind doors and windows and when they get a chance, curse them with words, thoughts or simply by looking with an envious eye.

They raise diseases to people, summon bears against cattle, spoil marital happiness, family, children, beauty, hunting traps and fishnets. They raise nightmares, remove sleep, send Night-Cryers to children to make them cry all night, hide graveyard dirt in a person's food to cause skin and eye diseases. With counterspells, the eyes of the envious are made to leak water, blood and lard.

> *Who looks with an envious eye,*
> *Glances with an eye askew,*
> *May their eyes leak water,*
> *One eye water, one eye blood,*
> *May their eyes rain sleet!*
> *I am a woman with an iron cap,*
> *I pull a sword from the sea,*

With which I'll smash your teeth,
And split your jaws!
Ancient Poems of the Finns

Enemy witches are exiled back to Northland and banished into the river, under the earth or inside the Iron Mountain. If they don't obey, the spellcaster threatens to find their mighty mother who was born before the night. This refers to Loviatar (Louhi) as the original witch mother.

There I will banish the witch,
There I will order the wizard,
Into the earth below my feet,
Nine fathoms deep,
There I will conjure the witch,
Into a rock in a stream,
If you still don't obey,
I will find thy mother,
Who was born before the night,
I will fetch thy mighty parent.
Ancient Poems of the Finns

Para

The Para is a witch's helper, created by the witch herself. It's a creature that brings good things to its owner, mainly milk and butter from neighbors' cows. The name comes from the Swedish word *bära* (to carry). The Para is the assistant of female witches. Male witches make their own assistant, the Tonttu (gnome), with similar tasks.

The Para can be made of different materials, but they must be stolen from someone. Its head is made of a ball of yarn and its three legs of the legs of a spinning wheel. The torso is made of stockings filled with bones taken from a corpse, usually the arm and finger bones. It has three eyes that are made of pearls.

One half of the Para's spirit comes from its owner and the other half from the owner's best cow. Its blood is created of the witch's own blood taken from her finger.

The Para is made in the witch's room at night with no-one else present. The ritual can also take place in a sauna, in a barn or at a river. The required components are put inside a sieve that is turned around at a fast pace while repeating a spell that brings the Para to life. Also a spinning wheel can be used.

The more times the spell is read, the stronger the Para will become. If someone sees or hears the ritual, the creation of the Para will fail.

Be born, be born, Para,
To carry butter and milk!
No-one is around to see,
No-one is around to hear,
Half of my body I will offer,
Half of my soul I will give.
Ancient Poems of the Finns

When the Para is born, it will ask the witch what she wishes it to carry. The witch gives it instructions to carry milk, butter, cream, grain, wool or even gold and silver. She tells the Para that it can only take orders from her, not from others.

The Para will suck milk from neighbors' cows. It carries the milk inside its mouth and belly and then vomits it into a bowl or a churn. Sometimes it's so full of milk that it has to vomit some of it on its way back, leaving little foam blobs in the grass.

The milk is mixed with blood because when the Para sucks milk from the cow, it also sucks its blood. The Para may be explicitly ordered to kill the neighbor's cow.

A Para can resemble an animal like a cat, a hare, a black bird or a frog, or look like an adult human being the size of a child. It can move unnoticed and silence dogs. It's kept happy by giving it porridge.

The Para and its owner have the same fate. If the Para is being harmed, so is the owner, and if the Para dies, its owner dies. This can happen if someone notices the Para stealing milk and hits it.

Not everybody succeeds in creating a Para. It takes a great witch to make one. There may be only one person in the village able to create it. If an incompetent person makes a Para, it can have the opposite effect. Instead of bringing milk and butter to the house, it will spoil all the milk and butter of its owner.

Part II: Deities of Death

Tuonela

Tuonela, the land of the dead, is situated on an island, separated from our world by a river. Tuoni (Death) brings the dead there, and Tuonetar (Lady of Death) receives them. The Daughter of Death is the gatekeeper, and the son guards the downstream.

The living are not allowed in, but great sages have visited the realm in search of a bride, wisdom from the dead or to bring a loved one back to life.

One must travel through three forests and three roads covered with axe blades before seeing the castles of Death shimmering in the distance.

The last obstacle is the Tuonela river. On the shore, one calls the Daughter of Death to bring a boat. She decides who is allowed to enter.

Daughter of Death

The Daughter of Death (Tuonen tytti) is a goddess of the underworld and the gatekeeper between the world of the living and the land of the dead. She's a maiden with black hair that glows like fire. With her sisters, she washes clothes at the riverbank and keeps watch.

If someone arrives at the opposite shore and calls her, she goes to meet them on her boat to bring them over the river to the island – but only if she's convinced they are truly dead.

Bring a boat, Tuoni's daughter,
Bring a ferry-boat, O maiden,
That may bear me o'er this channel,
O'er this black and fatal river.
Kalevala

The girl is responsible for not letting the living come to Tuonela. She interviews anyone trying to enter and is not easily fooled. Her interview is feared because she recognizes liars.

Girls of Death are scolding,
Maidens of Kalma reproaching:
"A boat will be brought,

If a reason is given,
What brought you to Tuonela,
Without a disease killing you,
Or other Surma defeating you."
Ancient Poems of the Finns

Usually Tuoni (Death) accompanies the dead to the underworld, and when they arrive, they have Death's hat on their head, his chains around their neck, mittens in their hands, bridles in their mouth and reins on their shoulders. From these signs, the gatekeeper knows the person is dead. Another sign is that Death is puffing from the person's mouth.

If someone arrives without Tuoni, it awakens the girl's suspicions, and she starts looking for signs that give out the cause of death: are the person's clothes wet, is their skin bloody, is their hair burnt.

When the living sage Väinämöinen arrives at the river and calls the girl, she wants to know the reason for him trying to enter Tuonela even though he looks alive.

Quick the daughter of Tuoni,
Magic maid of little stature,
Tiny virgin of Manala,
Tiny washer of the linen,
Tiny cleaner of the dresses,
At the river of Tuoni,
In Manala's ancient castles,
Speaks these words to Wainamoinen,
Gives this answer to his calling:
"Straightway will I bring the row-boat,
When the reasons thou hast given

Why thou comest to Manala,
In a hale and active body."
Kalevala

Väinämöinen has come to retrieve magic words from the dead but doesn't want to convey it for fear of not getting in. Instead, he tries to convince the girl that he's dead. He explains that after he died, Tuoni raised him from his coffin and brought him here. She doesn't believe him because in that case Tuoni would be with him, and he would have Tuoni's hat and gloves on.

"This a tale of wretched liars,
Had Tuoni brought thee hither,
Mana raised thee from the coffin,
Then Tuoni would be with thee,
Manalainen too would lead thee,
With Tuoni's hat upon thee,
On thy hands, the gloves of Mana."
Kalevala

Väinämöinen goes on to say that iron killed him, but the girl wonders why he is not bloody. Väinämöinen then says he drowned, but she can see his clothes are not wet. Väinämöinen says fire killed him. The girl answers that his eyebrows and beard would be burnt if this were true.

Väinämöinen has no choice but to confess the reason for his journey. Usually, if the girl detects a liar, she doesn't let them enter, in which case the visitor must use metamorphosis to get in, but in this case, she decides to make an exception. She brings him over the river but warns him that once a living person enters, they can never leave Tuonela.

"Thou art sure a stupid fellow,
Foresight wanting, judgment lacking,
Having neither wit nor wisdom,
Coming here without a reason,
Coming to Tuoni's empire,
Better far if thou shouldst journey,
To thy distant home and kindred,
Man they that visit Mana,
Few return from Mana's kingdom."
Kalevala

The daughter also performs the task of a grim reaper, rowing from shore to shore and entering houses to bring people with her to Tuonela. She travels either alone or with Tuoni, enters a home with her hair glowing, takes a sick family member from the bed and guides them to the black cabin of Death.

Tuoni's daughter, black hair,
Short maiden of Manala,
Rowed a shore, rowed another,
Under the ice, under the snow,
Rowed up to our shore,
Came Tuoni to our house,
Drew the curtain on the window,
Killed the father of the house,
Came with empty, left with full.
Ancient Poems of the Finns

Tuonetar, Lady of Death

Tuonetar (Lady of Death) is the female ruler of Tuonela, also called Tuonen akka (the Old Woman of Death). When Tuoni brings the dead to the underworld, Tuonetar receives them by offering them snake and lizard heads to eat, snake poison to drink and by putting them to sleep on a bed swarming with snakes and lizards.

> *There he was hosted,*
> *Given to eat,*
> *Given to drink,*
> *Poisons of snakes,*
> *Heads of lizards,*
> *Put to sleep,*
> *On a silk bed,*
> *Of snake poisons.*
> Ancient Poems of the Finns

Tucking people into bed, she promises they will only stay for six days, but in fact they stay there forever. She lures them to the underworld by saying they will get to sleep in a golden hall, but when the living relatives go look, they only see a pile of stones and black soil inside the grave.

Tuoni's old woman, hook-jaw,
Open mouthed queen of Manala,
Tucked in my father,
Lured him under the ground,
Promised death for six days,
Lost him for eternity.
Promised a golden grave,
Cast in copper,
When I went to look,
I saw a grave of black soil,
And a pile of stones.
Ancient Poems of the Finns

Tuonetar has iron fingers and iron nails, with which she spins her hair on a spinning wheel at the window of the Tuonela castle. She can also be seen sitting at the river with her three dogs Sulfur, Flame and Nameless dog who eat the broth of witches' curses.

Old Woman of Death, iron tooth,
Sits at the end of Deathland bridge,
Three dogs by her side,
One is Sulfur, the other is Flame,
The third is Nameless dog,
They bite the wrath of curses,
They lap the broth of curses.
Ancient Poems of the Finns

She can bring milk from under the ground if a witch has cursed a cow so that it doesn't give milk. Drops of milk are taken from the cursed cow, brought to the graveyard at night and put into a grave, and she is asked to give milk from Tuonela.

> *Old Woman of Death, dry-nail,*
> *Old woman under the earth,*
> *Bring my milk from Mana,*
> *The cow's givings from Tuonela.*
> Ancient Poems of the Finns

When living wizards travel to the underworld, Tuonetar welcomes them and offers them a pint of beer to drink. There's foam on top, but underneath, there are snakes, lizards, worms and maggots. When sage Väinämöinen arrives, she gives him a pint.

> *Tuonetar, the death-land hostess,*
> *Ancient hostess of Tuoni,*
> *Brings him pitchers filled with strong-beer,*
> *Fills her massive golden goblets,*
> *Speaks these measures to the stranger:*
> *"Drink, thou ancient Wainamoinen,*
> *Drink the beer of king Tuoni!"*
> Kalevala

The wizards usually notice the danger and fish out the snakes before drinking the beer. Väinämöinen inspects the drink, notices the animals and refuses to drink it.

Wainamoinen, wise and cautious,
Carefully inspects the liquor,
Looks a long time in the pitchers,
Sees the spawning of the black-frogs,
Sees the young of poison-serpents,
Lizards, worms, and writhing adders,
Thus addresses Tuonetar:
"Have not come with this intention,
Have not come to drink thy poisons,
Drink the beer of Tuonela."
Kalevala

Tuonetar wonders why he has come to Tuonela voluntarily. Väinämöinen tells her that he needs three magic words to complete a spell. Tuonetar refuses to give them to him, saying that Tuonela never gives out words. She also says that he will never leave Tuonela and puts him to sleep.

Spake the hostess, Tuonetar:
"Mana never gives these sayings,
Canst not learn them from Tuoni,
Not the lost-words of the Master;
Thou shalt never leave this kingdom,
Never in thy magic life-time,
Never go to Kalevala,
To Wainola's peaceful meadows.
To thy distant home and country."
Kalevala

Net Weavers

When Väinämöinen has been put to sleep, Tuonetar and the other dead gather on a rock in the river to weave fishnets to prevent him from escaping should he wake up.

The nets are made in a very short time, in a single night, but are gigantic in size and length, reaching up to a hundred or thousand fathoms long and wide.

> *Tuoni's three-fingered girl,*
> *A three-toothed crone*
> *Of the land of Lapps,*
> *Span a hundred fathom net*
> *On a single summer night.*
> Magic Songs of the Finns

Fishing nets in general are considered magical. They were originally created to catch the pike that had swallowed the first fire. A maggot of Death, Tuoni's grub, was found under the ground and burned in an iron boat. Its ashes were buried, and from the ashes grew flax that was used for the first nets. They were woven on a summer night on a rock in the water to give them power.

Instead of flax, the dead in Tuonela use iron to make their own nets. The weavers have crooked iron fingers and iron nails, and some have only three fingers, while others have one hundred fingers.

They spin iron yarn on a spinning wheel, weave the nets sitting on a rock and put them in the Tuonela river lengthwise and crosswise.

In Manala lived a woman,
In the kingdom of Tuoni,
Evil witch and toothless wizard,
Spinner of the threads of iron,
Moulder of the bands of copper,
Weaver of a hundred fish-nets,
Of a thousand nets of copper,
Spinning in the days of summer,
Weaving in the winter evenings,
Seated on a rock in water.
Kalevala

To escape from Tuonela, Väinämöinen changes himself into a snake and swims across the river. When the dead go look in the morning, there is no sight of him.

Like a snake among the willows,
Crawls he like a worm of magic,
Like an adder through the grasses,
Through the coal-black stream of death-land,
Through a thousand nets of copper
Interlaced with threads of iron,
From the kingdom of Tuoni,
From the castles of Manala.
Kalevala

Surma, Killer

Surma (death, killing) is a grim reaper who looks for people to bring with her to Tuonela. Also called Tappajainen (Killerling), she's a fine, tall lady in white clothes who rides a grey horse and is very thin because she lives without eating.

She's the daughter of Kalma, goddess of graves. When death is near, Surma opens her mouth and Kalma tilts her head, opening the door to her mansion.

To enter Surma's mouth means to die. She may sit at the end of the deathbed waiting to cut the lifeline. This is why nobody should stand at the end of the bed, only at the sides.

Through the kingdom of Tuoni,
To the end of Kalma's empire,
Where the jaws of Surma stand open,
Where the head of Kalma lowers,
Ready to devour the stranger,
To devour wild Lemminkainen;
But Tuoni cannot reach him,
Kalma cannot overtake him.
Kalevala

Surma walks, rides or skis along swamps and winter roads, wondering whom to kill in the next house: if she kills the grandfather, who will take care of fishing, if she kills the man of the house, who will plough the fields, if she kills the old lady, who will milk the cows, if she kills the young lady, who takes care of the children, if she kills the boy, the village maidens will cry, if she kills the girl, the suitors will cry.

Sometimes she can't decide whom to kill, at other times she decides to kill one or more of the family members. If a person's whole family dies, they wonder what they have done wrong to make Surma so mad that she did not take them, but only took the loved ones.

> *When have I, poor me,*
> *Maddened the mind of Surma,*
> *Tilted the mind of Kalma,*
> *If Surma had done right,*
> *If Kalma had done right,*
> *For Surma I would make socks,*
> *For Kalma's maiden gaiters.*
> Ancient Poems of the Finns

Surma can be summoned with magic songs to kill a chosen person. The singer mentions the name of the target person in the end of the song.

A daughter-in-law, who was bullied by her husband's family, took revenge by inviting Surma to kill the whole family: the father-in-law in the barn, the mother-in-law in the sauna, the sisters and brothers-in-law in the neighbor's house, the children on the floor and the grandfather on the stove.

> *Come, Surma, along the swamp,*
> *To kill the whole household,*

Kill the father-in-law in the barn,

The mother-in-law in the sauna,

The sister-in-law at a friend's door,

The brother-in-law in the neighbor's home,

Kill the children on the floor,

The old man on the stove.

Ancient Poems of the Finns

Surma is asked to come with an empty sack and leave with a full sack. Carrying an axe, she enters quietly wearing only socks so that no-one hears her approaching. As a reward, she's promised new socks and mittens, winter boots and a winter jacket.

Come, Surma, along the swamp,

Killerling, along the winter road,

Bring an empty sack,

Leave with a full sack!

For Surma I will sew socks,

Winter mittens for the Killer.

Ancient Poems of the Finns

She doesn't always come to kill someone, just to put children to sleep by wrapping a cloth around their eyes so that the mother can rest and have something to eat and drink. She may be asked to carry the child to her mansion as a guest to sleep.

Death Maidens

In lullabies, Death's maids and maidens are guardians of sleep. Chidren are lulled to sleep in a cradle in Tuoni's cabin where they get pampered, cuddled and sung to by the maidens. They may even get to walk around Death's mansion and herd Death's cattle.

Lull the child to Tuonela,
Lull to the cabins of Death,
To be lulled by Tuoni's old women,
To be held by Tuoni's maids,
To be cuddled by Tuoni's girls.
There it's good for the child to be,
At the cabins of Death's maidens,
To walk around the mansions,
To herd the cattle of Death.
Ancient Poems of the Finns

Tuoni's cabins are situated under the grass in earth's bosom. One enters by the roof made of peat, fish bones, pike teeth and bear palms. The back wall is made of deer bones, the sidewall of cricket bones, the door wall of apple trees and the door handle of weasel bones.

It's a golden mansion where the walls are smoothed with silk and the benches covered with silver. The floor is washed, the chairs are cast in copper and the golden tables filled with freshly baked bread.

> *There the roof is made of peat,*
> *The floor of small sand,*
> *And no Sun is shining in,*
> *And no wind is blowing,*
> *The walls are smoothed with silk,*
> *The benches covered with silver.*
> Ancient Poems of the Finns

Death's cabins are quiet. One doesn't hear a rooster's song, a dog's bark, a bird's voice, a shepherd's call, not even one's own mother's voice. It's dark and windless, no Sun is shining, no wind blowing, no rain dropping. The restless can finally rest among the long-shirts, flat-feet and moldy-mouths.

> *Lull the child to Tuonela,*
> *There the boy may lie,*
> *There the girl may rest,*
> *Among the long-shirts,*
> *Among the flat-feet,*
> *In the home of the moldy-mouths.*
> *No song of a rooster,*
> *No sound of a small bird.*
> Ancient Poems of the Finns

Anni, Death Bride

Anni is one of the daughters of Death. Her nicknames include black-brow, blue-hem, pearl-chest and fine-hair. Many suitors – ranging from ordinary men to the son of the Sun – have travelled to the underworld for her, but she hasn't agreed to marry anyone.

One suitor harnesses and saddles a hundred fiery horses, decorates them with gold and silver and takes with him a hundred swordsmen. Decided that he will rather try than stay without a partner, he rides a long way through three forests and roads to Tuonela.

When arriving, he sees Tuoni, Tuonetar and Anni sitting on an iron bench at the window of their mansion. They open the door and invite him in. The man asks to marry the daughter, and Tuoni or Tuonetar gives him three tasks in exhange for her.

> *I will only give my daughter,*
> *If you run the bloody mile,*
> *On the tips of needles,*
> *On the blades of knives,*
> *On the piles of axes.*
> Ancient Poems of the Finns

Possible tasks include running a road covered with sword blades, ploughing a snake field, chaining a bear and wolf, shooting a fiery pike, bathing in a fiery sauna with bloody water and forging an iron bridge, an iron horse or an eagle whose eyes shine like stars.

Many men have failed the tasks and died when, for example, running on the sword blades. But the man is victorious. He performs all tasks and is given Anni as wife.

The man returns to the world of the living with his bride. At home, he makes her a bed of wool to sleep in for one week, a bed of plumes for another week and a bed of eagle feathers for a third week.

But the girl starts to feel sick. The man asks her whether the horseback ride was exhausting or if her belt is too tight. She says the ride was fine and the belt is not tight, but she feels pressure in her heart, her head and her stomach. Her skin begins to rot.

The man hurries to a sorcerer to ask for advice. The witch says the girl will survive and he will find her perfectly healthy when he goes home.

When the man returns, he sees gravediggers digging a grave. He asks them who the grave is for, and they tell him they're building a home for the one who has last arrived. He goes in and finds out that Anni is already dead.

What are you building, my brother,
Are you carving war ships?
I am building a home for the dead,
A mansion for the departed.
Who has died at home?
Who has departed?
The one is dead at home,
The one has departed,
Who last has arrived.
Ancient Poems of the Finns

Kalma, Goddess of Graves

Kalma (corpse, tomb) is the goddess of graveyards. Graves are her mansions, beautiful homes, lovely houses, pinewood nests where it's pleasant to live and pass the time. Kalma opening the door to her mansion means someone is close to death, and when a person dies, Kalma holds them by one hand and Tuoni by the other.

> *It is good for thee to live,*
> *Pleasant for thee to pass the time*
> *In a house of fir, in a pinewood nest;*
> *Like a golden cuckoo thou wilt sing,*
> *Like a silver turtle-dove,*
> *In thy lofty home,*
> *In thy lovely house.*
> Magic Songs of the Finns

Kalma is summoned for various purposes: to ask for help or advice, to add to one's own power, for protection, to cure a disease, to beg for forgiveness or to ask her to come for support in a difficult situation.

Come, dread-inspiring Kalma,
Come at a time of anguish dire,
To give support, to safeguard me,
To help me and to strengthen me,
For the work that must be done,
The hurt that must be known about.
Magic Songs of the Finns

She's addressed in a respectful, even flattering way: kind Kalma, lovely Kalma, Kalma of the fair complexion, good Kalma, clean Kalma, the powerful force of Kalma. She's graceful as silk, white as flax, has silver ears, silver fingers, silver shoes and an iron sword.

Hear me golden Kalma,
Silver are your fingers,
Iron are your swords,
Silver are your shoes,
Golden you, Kalma,
White-blooded Kalma,
White are your fingers,
Silver are your ears.
Ancient Poems of the Finns

To talk to her, one goes to the graveyard at night, preferably alone, knocks the graves with a stick, asks if the dead are present, bows down, greets Kalma and utters the raising spell. It's possible to see her by taking an old skull from a grave and looking through its eyeholes.

Rise Kalma from the earth,
From the holy ground,
To my power, to my strength,
To my support, to my safety,
Graceful as silk, white as flax,
Arise big, arise small,
Arise all Kalma's folk!
Ancient Poems of the Finns

Once Kalma has risen, one can discuss the matter at hand with her. To carry some of her power, one takes soil, bones or small stones from the grave, puts them in a purse and gives a coin for her in exchange. Then, one asks Kalma to go back to repose in her mansion and leaves the graveyard without looking back.

Go back to your bed,
Go lie down in your mansion,
Go repose in your cradle.
Ancient Poems of the Finns

Bones and dirt taken from a grave contains Kalma's power. It can be used in weddings to protect the couple from witches who want to ruin the wedding. Sages put bones, teeth and dirt taken from a grave in a purse attached to their belt, and during the ceremony, circle the couple with an axe, a torch and a bottle of water to make the powers of iron, fire, water and death protect the couple.

Kalma is also a thief catcher. If money has been taken from a purse, it's burned, the ashes are put into a grave of an old corpse, the grave is hit with an axe, and Kalma is raised to go after the thief.

O Kalma, rise and bestir thyself,
To watch my thief,
To look after my goods,
To get my property,
To recover what is taken away,
With thy heavy, frightful hands,
With the chains of the Omnipotent.
Magic Songs of the Finns

If someone offends Kalma or her family by cursing, laughing, whistling, running or falling down on a graveyard, she sends out her wrath, a disease with symptoms varying from skin and eye disease to seizures, nightmares and insanity.

Strong healers are required to remove her wrath and banish it back to the grave. They lure it back by promising it delicacies like elbows, flesh and bones.

If thou hast bolted from a corpse (Kalma),
Into a corpse just disappear,
Go, Kalma, to a burial-ground,
To the edge of a holy field,
To the home of a man deceased,
To the house of a vanished one,
To the bed of one that has collapsed,
Under the rug of one that swooned.
There it is pleasant for thee to be,
Delightful 'tis for thee to live;
There thou hast bread of sifted flour,

Fat delicacies ready made,

Elbows enough are there

And much fat flesh for a hungry man to eat,

For one that longs for it to bite.

Magic Songs of the Finns

Pain Girl

Kiputyttö (Pain Girl) or Kivutar (Lady of Pain) is a healer goddess and an alleviator, remover and destroyer of pains. She's one of Death's daughters, responsible for collecting pains and hiding them inside the Pain Mountain (Kipuvuori) located in Tuonela at the intersection of three rivers.

On top of the mountain is a Pain Rock with nine holes, the middle one being the deepest. It has been pierced by the girl herself, and it leads nine fathoms deep inside the mountain.

Pain Girl, Maiden of Death,
In the middle of Pain Rock,
On the hill of Pain Mountain
Is gathering pains.
The rocks cry for pains,
The mountains moan.
Ancient Poems of the Finns

The rocks on the Pain Mountain are crying for pains, and the whole mountain is moaning. A snake inside the rock is whistling and inviting pains. There are dogs on the hill that used to be in pain but are now free of pain.

Wearing copper gloves, Pain Girl sits on the Pain Rock waiting for pains to arrive. They come from healers who, when healing a patient, plead her to make the suffering cease, seize the pains and bring them to the Pain Mountain.

> *Lovely old wife of pain!*
> *Good mistress, Kivutar,*
> *Come here where there is need of thee,*
> *Where a man is crying in distress.*
> *Come to see the sufferings,*
> *To seize the pains, to make the torment cease,*
> *To still the smarts in a poor human being's skin,*
> *In the body of a mother's son.*
> Magic Songs of the Finns

When the pains arrive, she collects them with a golden wing into a copper box, puts them in an iron kettle, boils them and pours them into the middle hole of the Pain Rock.

She stuffs the biggest pains in with a silver pole or turns the Pain Rock to grind them. The snake inside the rock eats some of the pains, and the rest travel nine fathoms deep, ending up in the cellars of Tuonela.

Once inside the mountain, they cannot get out. Pain Mountain can endure endless pain.

> *The centre hole is nine fathoms deep*
> *And into it the pains are flung,*
> *The dreadful sufferings are thrust,*
> *The dangerous wounds are cast by force,*
> *The calamities are pressed,*

So that by night they cannot act,
So that by day they can't escape.
Magic Songs of the Finns

Sometimes she rolls the pains into a ball and throws them into the Tuonela river or attaches them on the shoulders of pikes or salmons who will bring them to the deep sea.

If there are no pains in sight, Pain Girl suffers from pains herself. Holding her heart and belly, twisting her hands, scratching her chest and tearing her hair, she cries for pains. When receiving pains, she takes them in her arms and holds them against her chest before handing them over to the Pain Rock.

The girl of Tuoni, Maid of Pain,
Herself in pain was weeping tears,
Was lamenting in her suffering,
As she bustled about with
Her knees in hot ashes,
Her arms in the fire,
Collecting the pains
With stone gloves on her hands.
She boils the pains
And sickness in a wee kettle,
An iron baking pan,
At the end of an iron bench,
That no one should receive a pang,
That no one should receive a hurt.
Magic Songs of the Finns

Mother of Lemminkäinen

Strong healers can travel to Tuonela and change death to life. The mother of wizard Lemminkäinen is one of the most powerful sages in the Kalevala. She can communicate with the Sun, the Moon, trees and ravens and change herself into different animals. She knows the strongest healing spells and travels to the land of the dead to save her son.

She has taught him spells and initiated him into the art of magic by washing him with river water three times on a summer night and nine times on an autumn night.

My devoted mother washed me,
When a frail and tender baby,
Three times in the nights of summer,
Nine times in the nights of autumn,
That upon my journeys northward
I might sing the ancient wisdom,
Thus protect myself from danger;
When at home I sing as wisely
As the minstrels of thy hamlet.
Kalevala

She has foreseen the dangers of Lemminkäinen's journey to Northland and warned him about the northern witches and their magic. As a divination device, she has put his brush on the wall. If it starts bleeding, she will know he's in danger.

The failure to know the spell of a snake has led to the death of Lemminkäinen. A northern witch summoned a water snake through his heart, and since he didn't know the spell, he couldn't save himself but floated in the Tuonela river where the Son of Death cut him to pieces and threw his body parts into the river.

Lemminkäinen's mother notices that his brush is bleeding and immediately sets off to look for her son.

She travels to Northland to ask Louhi whether she knows anything about him. Louhi answers that maybe he was eaten by a wolf or a bear. The mother threatens Louhi with breaking the hinges of the magic mill if she doesn't reveal the whereabouts of her son. Louhi starts remembering that maybe she put him in a boat and he ended up in the maelstrom. Only when the mother threatens her with death, she reveals that she sent Lemminkäinen to shoot the swan of Tuonela.

The mother starts looking for Lemminkäinen, running through lands as a wolf, forests as a bear, marshes as a wild boar, seashores as a hare and waters as a wild duck.

Like the wolf she bounds through fenlands,
Like the bear, through forest thickets,
Like the wild-boar, through the marshes,
Like the hare, along the sea-coast,
To the sea-point, like the hedgehog
Like the wild-duck swims the waters,
Casts the rubbish from her pathway,
Tramples down opposing brush-wood,
Stops at nothing in her journey

Seeks a long time for her hero,
Seeks, and seeks, and does not find him.
Kalevala

She talks with trees, the Moon and the Sun to know if they have seen Lemminkäinen, and the Sun tells her that he has died in the dark river of Death.

In anguish, the mother goes to blacksmith Ilmarinen and asks him to forge a rake that can be used to rake the deep river of Tuonela. Ilmarinen forges a copper rake with a handle five hundred fathoms long and iron teeth a hundred fathoms long.

Lemminkäinen's mother hurries to the river, pleads the Sun to put the inhabitants of Tuonela to sleep and starts raking the waters. At first, she doesn't find anything, but when she moves further downstream, Lemminkäinen's shirt gets stuck in the rake's teeth, then his stockings and his hat.

She rakes further, and Lemminkäinen's ring finger and left toe are caught upon the rake. Pulling him to the surface, she notices that he's missing one arm, half a head and many other body parts and wonders whether she could make him alive again.

A raven hears her and says that she cannot bring him to life because a whitefish has already eaten his eyes and a pike has split his shoulders. She should just throw his parts into the river and let him turn into a cod or a whale.

But the mother will not give up on her son. Once more, she rakes the river and finds a hand, half a backbone, another half of a ribcage and the other parts.

She starts building his body anew by placing the parts together bone to bone, flesh to flesh, joint to joint and vessel to vessel and summons Suonetar, Goddess of Veins, to help her.

Once Lemminkäinen's body is back together, life returns to him, but he still can't talk. His mother orders a bee to fly to a far-away forest beyond nine seas and bring back healing ointments that she uses on him. Then she utters the spell that brings him back to life.

Wake, arise from out thy slumber,
From the worst of low conditions,
From thy state of dire misfortune!
Kalevala

She wants to know how he died, and he tells her what happened and that he didn't know the spell of the snake. The mother wonders why he had bragged about using magic on Northland witches when he didn't even know the snake spell.

Spake again the ancient mother:
"O thou son of little insight,
Senseless hero, fool-magician,
Thou didst boast betimes thy magic
To enchant the wise enchanters,
On the dismal shores of Lapland,
Thou didst think to banish heroes,
From the borders of Pohyola;
Didst not know the sting of serpents,
Didst not know the reed of waters,
Nor the magic word-protector!
Learn the origin of serpents,
Whence the poison of the adder."
Kalevala

Ladies of Veins, Flesh and Membranes

Suonetar (Lady of Veins) is a healer goddess who sits on an iron bench and spins her copper spinning wheel to create new blood vessels.

If someone is injured, she takes a bundle of veins under her arm, goes to the patient, replaces broken veins with new ones, knits them together with a silver needle, sets the vessels in their place, joins the venules and closes the wounds.

Who knotted up the veins,
Prepared with magic words the threads?
The beauteous woman Suonetar,
The lovely spinner of the veins,
On a splendid spinning-wheel,
On a copper spindle-shank,
On the top of a golden stool,
At the end of an iron bench,
She knotted up the veins
And the threads prepared with magic words.
Magic Songs of the Finns

In the Kalevala, she assists the mother of Lemminkäinen in weaving her son's body parts back together.

> *Suonetar, thou slender virgin,*
> *Goddess of the veins of heroes,*
> *Skilful spinner of the vessels,*
> *With thy slender, silver spindle,*
> *With thy spinning-wheel of copper,*
> *Set in frame of molten silver,*
> *Come thou hither, thou art needed;*
> *Bring the instruments for mending,*
> *Firmly knit the veins together,*
> *At the end join well the venules,*
> *In the wounds that still are open,*
> *In the members that are injured.*
> *Kalevala*

Suonetar usually works together with Kalvotar (Lady of Membranes) and Lihatar (Lady of Flesh) who prepare new membranes and flesh and bring them to the injured. Suonetar ties up the broken veins, Kalvotar repairs the membranes and Lihatar attaches the flesh to the bones.

> *Suonetar, slender maiden,*
> *Walking, strolling,*
> *A bundle of veins under her arm,*
> *Kalvotar, slender maiden,*
> *Walking, strolling,*

A bundle of membranes under her arm,
Lihatar, slender maiden,
Walking, strolling,
A bundle of flesh under her arm,
Where veins have collapses,
There new veins are tied,
Where membranes are broken,
There new membranes are grown,
Where flesh has vanished,
There new flesh is attached.
Ancient Poems of the Finns

Part III: Nature Goddesses

Sky

The sky is the home of the air and wind goddesses. The Luonnotars (Naturesses) are nature goddesses who may sit on rainbows and sky domes or descend to the earth to walk on seashores, making observations, giving advice and discussing things they see.

In the Kalevala, Ilmatar (Lady of the Air) becomes a water maiden, gets impregnated by the wind and gives birth to Väinämöinen.

The wind goddesses live at the North Pole. Tuuletar is the goddess of wind, Viimatar the goddess of gale and Etelätär the goddess of the south wind who protects cattle on pastures by taking them in her arms.

Nature's old wife, Etelätär,
Pray bring thy horn from further off,
From the centre of the sky;
From the sky a honeyed horn.
Magic Songs of the Finns

The sky is the birthplace of powerful beings like the bear, fire, iron, gold and silver.

Lady Moon and Lady Sun

Gold and silver are magical metals of the gods. The Sun is associated with silver and the Moon with gold. Kuutar (Lady of the Moon) and Päivätär (Lady of the Sun) are goddesses who sit on rainbows spinning gold and silver threads from their hair, weaving fabrics on a silver spinning wheel and making garments. Lady Sun spins the threads and Lady Moon knits the fabrics. Otavatar, goddess of the seven stars, sometimes helps them. They also make gold and silver jewelry.

I heard Lady Moon knitting,
I heard Lady Sun weaving,
I went to Lady Moon,
I reached Lady Sun,
Lady Moon gave her gold,
Lady Sun gave her silver,
I put the gold on my brow,
The good silver on my belt,
To shimmer as gold,
To shine as silver.
Ancient Poems of the Finns

If one sees them weaving and approaches them, they may drop garments and jewelry from the sky to be worn, for example, at weddings. The garments they make have magical qualities. Sorcerers who need protective gear ask them to weave a cape, blanket or shirt to sleep under during the night and wear during the day to make them immune to curses.

Sages who conduct wedding ceremonies and protect the couple from witches wear garments and jewelry made by the goddesses: a gold and silver shirt, belt, gloves, rings, bracelets and hair pieces.

Weave me a cloth of gold,
Rattle me out a silver cloth,
Make ready a defensive shirt,
Prepare a copper cloak
Under which I'll stay at night,
Which I can wear by day,
When that sorcerer is throwing spells.
Magic Songs of the Finns

They make clothes for other nature goddesses. The gold and silver dress offered to water goddess Vellamo in exchange for fish is woven by Kuutar and Päivätär. They also make bread and cakes to be offered to forest goddess Mielikki.

In the Kalevala, the mother of a girl named Aino meets the goddesses as a child when she is wandering on the mountains.

The mother receives from them gold and silver shirts, skirts, belts, socks, rings, necklaces and bracelets, wears them for three days and puts them in a box. She hasn't seen them since childhood because she's saving them for her daughter.

But Aino never gets married. She goes to the water and becomes a mermaid. The mother cries so much that her tears create three rivers.

"Give thy silver, Moon's fair daughters,
To a poor, but worthy maiden;
Give thy gold, O Sun's sweet virgins,
To this maiden, young and needy."
Thereupon the Moon's fair daughters
Gave me silver from their coffers;
And the Sun's sweet shining virgins
Gave me gold from their abundance,
Gold to deck my throbbing temples,
For my hair the shining silver.
Kalevala

When Kuutar and Päivätär give away gold and silver, they start crying. Their tears fall to the earth so that in the morning, one can see droplets of water in the grass. From their tears, oak trees are born.

Kuutar bewailed her gold,
Her silver Päivätär,
A tear trickled from her eyes,
A water-drop rolled down
On her lovely face,
From her lovely face
To her swelling breast,
From there it rolled into a dell;
From it a lovely oak sprang up..
Magic Songs of the Finns

Blacksmith Ilmarinen even tries to forge a woman of these celestial metals. His wife's death has brought such grief and sorrow to him that he can't even forge anymore, and all he does is cry.

One day, he goes to the ocean to gather gold and silver from the water, brings them to his smithy and puts them into the furnace.

After days of failed attempts, he adds more gold and silver, and finally, a woman arises from the fire, golden-haired, silver-headed, beautiful in form and feature.

Other people are scared of her, calling her a golden ghost. Ilmarinen tries to bring her to life and forges her feet, hands and arms.

But the bride is lifeless. Her feet are not walking, her arms do not embrace him, her ears are not hearing, her mouth not speaking, her eyes not seeing.

He lays her on a silk couch, prepares a bath for her and tries to keep her warm with bear skins and wool blankets, but his efforts are in vain. The bride of gold and silver remains lifeless.

From the fire a virgin rises,
Golden-haired and silver-headed,
Beautiful in form and feature.
All are filled with awe and wonder,
But the artist and magician.
Ilmarinen, metal-worker,
Forges nights and days unceasing,
On the bride of his creation;
Feet he forges for the maiden,
Hands and arms, of gold and silver;
But her feet are not for walking,
Neither can her arms embrace him.
Ears he forges for the virgin,

But her ears are not for hearing;
Forges her a mouth of beauty,
Eyes he forges bright and sparkling;
But the magic mouth is speechless,
And the eyes are not for seeing.
Kalevala

Panutar, Fire Maiden

Panutar (Lady of Fire) or Fire Maiden (*tulen tyttö*), is a goddess of air and the mother of fire. She belongs in the family of three great powers: water, fire and iron. Of these powers, water is the oldest son, and fire and iron are the younger daughters. Whereas water was born in the mountain, fire and iron were born in the sky.

Panutar was sitting on the highest sky dome weaving gold and silver fabrics. Ukko, the thunder god, struck the first fire with his sword and gave the spark to the goddess. She lulled it above the clouds in a golden cradle with silver straps, becoming the Fire Maiden, the mother of fire.

Fire was born in the sky,
On the Seven Stars' back,
There fire was rocked,
Dear flame was swung
In a golden copse,
On the top of a golden knoll.
Kasi, the beautiful young girl,
The fire-maiden of the sky,
'Tis she that rocked the fire,
Swung to and fro the flame

In the centre of the sky,
Above nine skies;
The cords of silver shook,
The golden hook gave a creak
While the girl was rocking the fire,
While swinging to and fro the flame.
Magic Songs of the Finns

But the restless fire spark jumped out of the cradle and fell down to earth through nine skies, burning people along the way and landing in a child's cradle. The child's mother, who knew how to charm fire, grabbed it, turned it into a bundle and threw it into the Deathland river where a pike swallowed it.

The fiery spark fell suddenly,
The red drop whizzed,
Through the heavens flashed,
Through the clouds fell down
From above the nine skies,
Through the six speckled firmaments.
Magic Songs of the Finns

To catch the pike, nature goddesses started weaving fishnets, and magicians with iron gloves were summoned. A golden-headed and silver-bladed knife was dropped from the sky, with which sage Väinämöinen cut the pike's stomach open and released the fire to be used by humankind from then on.

Even though fire was tamed in the beginning of time, it can get wild anytime. The sparks being Fire Maiden's daughters and sons, she must keep them in control and discipline them if needed. She's called to help when fighting fires.

> Fire girl, Fire maiden,
> Golden king of fire,
> Come to get your own,
> Come to collect your arrows,
> Come to pick up your sons!
> Ancient Poems of the Finns

She tames the sparks by shaking her skirt and hiding them in her furs and clothes and then heals the burns by eating the broth of fire from the wounds.

> O Panutar, best girl,
> When needed hither come
> To quench a fire,
> To reduce a flame;
> Give thy skirts a shake,
> Make their borders sway,
> Put the fire in thy furs,
> The flame in thy clothes,
> Throw it into thy rags,
> Keep it safe in thy ragged clothes.
> Magic Songs of the Finns

Iron

Iron is the youngest sister of the three powers iron, fire and water. She originates from the sky and Luonnotars, nature goddesses, are her mothers.

Water is the oldest brother,
Iron the youngest sister,
Fire the middle one.
Ancient Poems of the Finns

Three Luonnotars were walking on the sky dome with swollen breasts that began to ache so much that they had to start milking them. The milk poured down from the sky to the earth.

They milked three different milks. The eldest goddess gave black milk, the second one red milk and the youngest one white milk. The black milk grew into soft iron, the red became brittle iron and the white became steel.

Three maidens were born,
All the three Luonnotars,
To be mothers of iron ore,
To be generators of steel.

The girls came swinging along,
'Long the edge of the air the maidens stepped
With swollen breasts, with smarting teats,
On the ground they milked their milk,
Let their breasts pour forth,
They milked upon land,
They milked upon swamps,
On still waters they milked.
One milked black milk,
She was the eldest of the girls,
The second discharged a jet of red,
She of the girls was the middle one,
The third poured forth white milk,
She was the youngest of the girls.
One had milked black milk,
From it soft iron had its origin,
One had discharged a jet of red,
Thence brittle iron was obtained,
One had poured forth white milk,
And from it steel was made.
Magic Songs of the Finns

Iron got scared of her sister, the fire, who had gone wild, burning down lands and forests and threatening to burn her too. She fled into a swamp where she spent years hiding in the cold water under roots and tree stumps. Bears and wolves were roaming on the swamp, and in their footsteps, iron surfaced. A blacksmith found her, took her to his smithy and started to forge the first swords and tools. Suffering in the flames of the furnace, iron promised to never harm a human if she ever got out. But then a hornet, sent by the Hiisi goblins, poisoned the quenching water. Iron became evil and started to cut people in the form of swords, knives and axes.

> Then wretched Iron shouted out
> "Oho! thou smith Ilmarinen,
> Take me away from here,
> From the torments of angry Fire."
> Magic Songs of the Finns

From then on, if a weapon or tool has made a wound, iron is reminded of her origin inside the swamp and the breasts of the Luonnotars and scorned for suddenly growing so big and bold that she started to do evil deeds. At the same time, since she's not considered inherently evil, she's appeased by reminding her that she wouldn't be malicious if the Hiisi had not poisoned the water.

> Thou wast not great in former days,
> Not great nor small,
> When thou as milk didst lie,
> As fresh milk didst repose
> In a young maiden's teats,
> Wast growing in a maiden's breast,
> On a long bank of cloud,
> Under the level sky.
> Magic Songs of the Finns

Auteretar, Mist Maiden

The Mist Maiden (*terhen neiti*) is an air goddess of mist, fog and haze, also called Fog Girl (Ututyttö) or Lady of Haze (Auteretar). Her son Auterinen is the god of the steam of the sauna that has healing qualities.

Auteretar has a sieve with which she sprinkles mist down from the sky to the forest and the sea to cover and hide animals and even whole ships inside the fog.

> *Mist maiden, maid of fog,*
> *Air maiden Auteretar!*
> *With a sieve sift mist,*
> *Keep scattering fog,*
> *From the sky let fall thick fog,*
> *Lower a vapour from the air*
> *On the clear surface of the sea,*
> *On the wide-open main.*
> Magic Songs of the Finns

In hunting, she may be asked to cover a bear, a deer or a bird with mist so that it doesn't see the approaching hunters. Blacksmith Ilmarinen summons her in the Kalevala to hide the bear and wolf of Death inside fog so that he can capture them and bring them to Louhi.

> *"Terhenetar, ether-maiden,*
> *Daughter of the fog and snow-flake,*
> *Sift the fog and let it settle*
> *O'er the bills and lowland thickets,*
> *Where the wild-bear feeds and lingers,*
> *That he may not see my coming,*
> *May not hear my stealthy footsteps!"*
> *Terhenetar hears his praying,*
> *Makes the fog and snow-flake settle*
> *On the coverts of the wild-beasts;*
> *Thus the bear he safely bridles,*
> *Fetters him in chains of magic,*
> *In the forests of Tuoni,*
> *In the blue groves of Manala.*
> Kalevala

Auteretar can be summoned against enemies at sea to either hide the enemy boat inside fog so that they can't move or to cover one's own boat to hide it from the enemy.

In the Kalevala, Louhi orders her to spread a fog around the ship of the sages who have stolen her mill. The maiden creates a fog that traps their ship for three days.

"Daughter of the morning-vapors,
Sift thy fogs from distant cloud-land,
Sift the thick air from the heavens,
Sift thy vapors from the ether,
On the blue-back of the broad-sea,
On the far extending waters,
That the ancient Wainamoinen,
Friend of ocean-wave and billow,
May not baffle his pursuers!"
Kalevala

They are only freed when Väinämöinen strikes the water with his magic sword to make the fog break and rise back to the sky.

Forest

A myriad of gods and goddesses rule the different areas of the forest. The main gods Tapio and Mielikki are responsible for the whole realm, while the many daughters, sons, maids and workers of their household have their own areas, whether it's a swamp, thicket, heath or a specific tree. The gods protect their realm and its animals. When entering the forest, the gods and goddesses of the different areas are greeted.

Old Man of the Forest,
Old Woman of the Forest,
Maids of the Forest,
Boys of the Forest,
Beautiful Workers of the Forest,
Greybeard of the Forest,
Golden King of the Forest,
Industrious Hostess of the Forest,
Blue-caped Woman of the Wilderness,
Red-sock Hostess of the Swamp,
Beautiful Hostess of the Heath.
Ancient Poems of the Finns

Mielikki

Mielikki is the main forest goddess, Hostess of the Woods (*metsän emäntä*), who takes care of the forest and guards the golden gates of her realm.

She's assisted by the many forest daughters and sons, including the goddesses of trees Hongatar (Lady of the Pine), Tuometar (Lady of the Bird Cherry), Katajatar (Lady of the Juniper) and Pihlajatar (Lady of the Rowan).

> *The distinguished woman Suvetar,*
> *Wood's daughter-in-law, the Mielikki,*
> *The kindly mistress Hongatar,*
> *Pihlajatar the little lass,*
> *Katajatar the lovely girl,*
> *And Tapio's daughter Tuometar,*
> *As my shepherds I shall send*
> *And make them into godmothers.*
> Magic Songs of the Finns

Forest animals are under her protection. She guides their walk with blue ribbons and threads made of her hair. She's one of the godmothers of the bear and has given them claws and teeth.

Mielikki dresses up in golden skirts, bracelets, rings and earrings, wears plates of gold in her hair and golden ringlets in her locks. When she appears like this, it means she's in a favourable mood and lets hunters enter the forest.

For hunting luck, they offer her gold and silver and ask her to change her twig clothes into a fancy dress. The offerings are placed on the table of the forest, a flat fir tree.

Mielikki makes the whole forest beautiful by dressing alder trees in lovely clothes, decking the pines with gold, putting flowers on the heads of pines and silver on the heads of firs and girding copper belts around old pines and silver belts around firs.

The arms of the forest's mistress,
Of the kindly mistress Mielikki
Had golden bracelets on,
On her fingers golden rings,
On her head were plates of gold,
On her hair wee flowers of gold,
In golden ringlets were her locks,
Pendants of gold were in her ears,
Her skirts were hung with golden tags,
Around her neck were goodly pearls.
The kindly mistress then,
The pleasant mistress of the woods
Was well disposed to give her gifts,
Indulgent with her largesses.
Magic Songs of the Finns

Once the forest is ready, she takes the golden keys from the ring at her side, opens the gate and lets the animals roam toward the hunters. She hits hills and valleys with a golden axe to mark the path.

The forest daughters may stand in for Mielikki in her tasks. Annikki, the tiny forest maiden, is the highest ranking daughter and has nine maids. She sits on a golden stool at a fiery stream with golden keys in her hand. She blows a whistle to wake up the animals and puts a silk scarf as a bridge over the river for them. Tuulikki, forest daughter, guides the animals with a fir branch to make them run faster, and Tellervo, shepherdess of the forest, guides them with a whip of mountain ash.

Any goddess can send out a disease, the wrath of the forest, if someone offends them by making noise in the forest, falling down or getting frightened by an animal. The disease can manifest as sore eyes, skin eruptions, boils, vomiting and nausea.

Mielikki can help remove the wrath. The healer goes to the forest at night and washes the patient with a mixture of swamp water, bird feathers, twigs from an ant nest and bones of a bird killed by an eagle. The remaining water is poured over tree roots. Mielikki is given offerings and asked for forgiveness.

Mielikki, girl of the forest,
You wise wife of the woods,
I did a bad thing,
When visiting your home,
Please accept the good,
And give away my bad.
Ancient Poems of the Finns

Hongatar, Lady of the Pine

Hongatar (Lady of the Pine) is one of the forest goddesses who raised the bear. She has a special place in bear myths because the life cycle of the bear is tied to her territory, the pine tree.

According to the myth, the bear was born in the sky, near the Sun and the Moon, on the shoulders of the seven stars of the Great Bear. There was a fire flash, and the bear emerged. The maidens of the air took care of the newborn. They put it in a golden cradle, let it down to earth and hung it on a pine branch.

In its forest castle, the bear was rocked and swayed, nursed and raised by the Lady of the Pine, the Lady of the Bird Cherry, the Lady of the Juniper and the Lady of the Rowan.

> *Where was broad-forehead born,*
> *Was honey-paws produced?*
> *There was broad-forehead born,*
> *Was honey-paws produced,*
> *Close to the moon, beside the sun,*
> *On the shoulders of Charles's Wain.*
> *From there was he let down to earth,*
> *To a honeyed thicket's edge,*
> *To be nursed by Hongatar,*

To be rocked by Tuometar,
At the root of a stunted fir,
Under an aspen's branching head,
On the edge of the forest-fort,
In the home of the golden wilderness...
Sinisirkku, the forest maid, rocked him,
Swayed him to and fro in a cradle of gold,
In silver straps, under a fir with branching crown,
Under a bushy pine.
Magic Songs of the Finns

It was given its name at a fiery rapids. Right from the beginning, it had many pet names: honey-paws, forest beauty, forest gold, forest apple, broad-forehead, broad-paws.

Growing up, the bear still had no teeth and claws, but once it was old enough, its godmother Mielikki gave them to it for a promise to never harm a human. Whenever a bear is threatening or attacking, it's reminded of its heavenly origin and the promise it made to the forest goddess.

Hongatar and the other goddesses continue to take care of the bear. It's a pet of the forest maidens and should not be disrespected. In return, the goddesses tell their beloved honey-paws not to commit evil acts against people or cattle.

One can ask for Hongatar's protection when walking in the forest or shepherding cattle. She guides the bear away from pastures and tells it to hide its claws inside its fur and its muzzle inside moss so that it doesn't even hear the cattle. She may wrap a rowan band around its muzzle and even shepherd the cattle herself to keep it protected.

If a bear has done an evil deed, Hongatar is called to take responsibility for its actions.

Good mistress, Hongatar,
Observant woman, Tapiotar,
Come, when thou art needed, here, approach,
When thou art summoned here,
The evil actions of thy son,
Thy child's outrageous deeds to see.
Here damage has come to pass,
An accident occurred,
Thy son has done an evil deed,
Thy child an act of villany;
The villain broke his oath,
Ate his honour like a dog,
When he took to evil acts,
Began committing hideous deeds.
Magic Songs of the Finns

Bear hunting is only allowed if the goddesses allow it. It's an intricate ritual consisting of preparation, greeting the forest, asking for permission to enter, asking goddesses to show the way to the bear, waking up the bear, killing the bear, having a feast and returning the bear to the forest.

After a successful hunt, the bear's skull and bones are carried back to the forest in a procession. The skull is hung on the branch of Hongatar, and the rest of the bones are buried under her roots. The bear has returned in spirit to its home, to the lap of the Lady of the Pine.

Lady of the Swamp

The Lady of the Swamp (*suon emäntä*) possesses the power of both forest and water. She often appears together with the goddesses of heaths and thickets.

They are addressed with nicknames red-sock, blue-sock, yellow-shoe or blue-cape: Blue-cape Old Woman of Thickets, Beautiful Hostess of the Heath, Red-sock Lady of the Swamp.

These goddesses have bone fingers and steel jaws. They can be raised to fight witches and the envious.

> *Bone-finger, rise from the brook,*
> *Steel-jaw from the sludge,*
> *To curse the witches,*
> *To knock over the envious!*
> Ancient Poems of the Finns

Swamps are roaming areas of bears and wolves, and the Lady of the Swamp controls the animals in her area. When cows pasture in the forest, she puts her bears in iron chains and her wolves in bridles to protect them.

Blue-sock Lady of the Swamp,
Blue-sock, yellow-shoe,
Keep the bears in iron chains,
Keep the wolves in bridles!
Ancient Poems of the Finns

If bird hunters make her in a favorable mood, she may open the gate to the swamp and make a path for them to walk on. Her seven key maids help her open the gates, and the other goddesses guide the animals' run by putting ribbons over the water as bridges.

Old Lady of the Forest,
Blue-caped Old Woman of Thickets,
Red-sock Lady of the Swamp,
Beautiful Hostess of the Heath.
Put a blue ribbon,
Across the Northland river,
For the animals to run.
Ancient Poems of the Finns

The Lady of the Swamp is connected to the birth of healing ointments. She was combing her hair with a golden brush when one hair fell into the water, giving birth to a young maiden who rose to land on a nameless field and lay down to sleep. She never woke up, and hay started growing on her. From this hay, the first balms were made.

She can fight both fire and frost. If fire has done damage, she brings frost from the swamp on the burns to alleviate pain and captures the fire by wrapping it inside her skirts to cool it off.

Rise from the dell, dear Maid!
From the gravel, thou clean-faced one,
Blue-socks! from the corner of a swamp,
Red laces! from a dale;
From the stream raise frost,
From the swamp some cooling stuff
For the places that are burnt,
For the fearful scars from fire,
In thy folds wrap up the fire,
In thy skirts the flame,
In thy clean dress,
In thy white clothes.
Magic Songs of the Finns

If the frost attacks and charm spells are not enough to tame it, she is summoned to destroy its path and put a stop to its journey.

The great woman from the swamp I'll raise,
The stout old mother from the mire,
Who will destroy thy path,
Will bring on thy journey evil things.
Magic Songs of the Finns

Käreitär

Forest goddesses are original mothers (*emuu*) of animals. Hillervo is the mother of the otter, Höyheneukko the mother of birds and Tyytikki the mother of squirrels.

Käreitär is the mother of foxes. Foxes are messengers, animals of metamorphosis and witches' familiars that can be summoned to fight animals conjured by another witch. To run unnoticed in the woods, witches turn themselves into a fox.

Nature goddesses send foxes to the forest to fetch magical ingredients. When Osmotar, goddess of beer, was brewing the first beer, she sent a fox to the woods to get honey.

Foxes run to inform people if someone has drowned in a lake or died in the forest, even though they are untrustworthy because they can eat the ducks on the yard instead.

Who then tell the cruel story,
Who will bear the evil tidings.
To the cottage of her sister?
Will the fox repeat the story
Tell the tidings to her sister?
Nay, the fox must not be herald,
He would eat the ducks and chickens.
Kalevala

Käreitär is addressed when hunting foxes. She opens the forest gates, guides the fox and is offered gold, silver or salt in exchange for a permission to hunt. She puts the gold in her cup and the silver in her goblet.

> *Käreitär, golden wife,*
> *Tinatti mother of forest,*
> *Take the gold in your cup,*
> *Put the silver in your goblet.*
> Ancient Poems of the Finns

She is persuaded to accept the offerings by explaining her that the bits of gold are as old as the Moon and the bits of silver are as old as the Sun.

> *O chosen woman, Kunnotar,*
> *O golden woman, Kärehetär,*
> *Come away from melting gold,*
> *From smelting silver come away;*
> *In thy bowl I put bits of gold,*
> *Bits of silver in thy cup,*
> *These bits of gold are as old as the Moon,*
> *The bits of silver as old as the Sun.*
> Magic Songs of the Finns

Black foxes have their own goddess, Lukutar. They are fire foxes that shine in the dark and are believed to create northern lights by sweeping snowy hills with their tail. Northern lights are in Finnish called *revontulet*, fires of the fox.

For hunters, fire foxes are the most valuable ones. Gold and silver are put on the branches of fir trees as offerings to Lukutar when placing traps.

Forest Maiden

People who go to the forest may encounter the Forest Maiden (*metsänneito*). Looking like a beautiful woman from the front, she approaches campfires to warm herself up or to dance around the fire. Only when seeing her back, one realizes she's not human.

A hunter put on a fire in the forest to cook food. A woman in fancy clothes approached it to warm up her hands but didn't speak. The man said, "You can come closer", but the woman turned around, and that's when the man noticed her back was a decayed tree stump.

Two men were chopping wood when they saw an extremely beautiful lady run between the trees, fast like the wind. After a while, she ran back, and the men saw that she didn't have a backside at all, only a hollow bark of an old fir tree.

The maiden protects people by warning them of snakes, bears and falling trees. A man was sleeping in the forest when he heard someone whisper, "Wake up! An old man is being buried!" When he got up, a tall tree fell right at the spot where he had been sleeping.

She may give presents to those who are kind to her. A man was chopping wood when the weather suddenly turned cold. He made a fire and left it on. The maiden came at the fire and thanked him for not putting it off so the goddesses could keep warm.

She gave him a white shirt and said, "Do not tell anyone who gave you this shirt. If you tell one single person, I will take it away". The man kept the shirt for many years everywhere he went but never told anyone.

It was always clean and never had to be washed. One day, he told someone how he got it, and immediately, it vanished into thin air.

The goddess may even give her pets, forest animals, to hunters. A hunter saw her skirt catching fire and shouted for her to watch out. The thankful maiden promised him her best pig, and the next day, he caught a big bear.

Another hunter made a fire and started eating. The maiden approached him looking hungry, and he gave her some food. She said, "You are a good man. I will make my best ox approach you." In the morning, he saw a big elk in front of him.

A third hunter saw her but didn't give her food, just cursed at her. She said she will send him her best dog. In the morning, a large bear came toward him. His weapon didn't work, and the bear attacked him. He barely stayed alive.

Ajatar

Ajatar or Ajattara is a forest goddess who lures people to the forest and makes them get lost. She can cause nightmares or appear as one. Her name comes from *ajaa* (to chase, drive, pursue).

Nightmare can appear in the form of a fox or an old lady in black clothes, causing anxiety, restless sleep, bad dreams and sleepwalking. She can sit on the chest of the sleeping person pressing herself so hard on them that they cannot move, scream, wake up or breathe properly. If in an angry mood, she can press so hard that the person will die.

Ajatar or another forest goddess can make people and animals get lost in the forest by throwing a blanket or cover on them so that they don't find their way out. The forest cover (*metsänpeitto*) is an upside down world where nothing is as it was before. If someone comes to look for the lost one, they cannot see them or hear their voice even if they walk right past them. The person may be frozen in a stone-like state, and the searchers sit on the stone but still don't see them.

A girl was put under forest cover. The whole village looked for her, but she was nowhere to be found. A sorcerer was consulted, and she revealed the place to find her. Afterwards, the girl told her family that she had heard her mother crying and shouting her name and seen the people who were looking for her. They were so close that the hem of a searcher's shirt had touched her, but the forest goddess had warned her not to speak.

Another girl got lost in the forest. For two weeks, she was sitting between the roots of a fallen tree. Forest gods in the form of little girls and boys brought her food every day. It was very tasty meat.

When the girl complained that her feet were cold, the gods warmed them up. As she finally got out and her family went to look where she had been, they only found frog bones and frog meat between the roots.

When putting cows out to pasture in the spring, prayers are spoken to protect them from Ajatar's mischief and forest maidens' pranks. If an animal has been lured to the forest and stayed under the forest cover for one or two days, it becomes invisible to human eye and looks like a rock or a pile of earth. One can test whether the animal is still alive by shouting at the forest. If an echo comes back, it's still alive.

To release someone from the forest cover, a passageway can be made by raising the roots of a tree. Once the gate is ready, one steps on a rock and shouts a spell to the gods to release their prisoner.

> *Host of the forest,*
> *Hostess of the forest,*
> *Golden king of the forest,*
> *Release your prisoner!*
> Ancient Poems of the Finns

The culprit is not always a forest goddess but a witch. Once, a witch got revengeful because some village boys were teasing her. She cursed their families' cows to make them run to the forest and stay there for several days. In these kind of cases, a sage is usually needed to read the necessary counterspells to try and lure the cattle from the forest or to confront the witch head-on.

Mountain

Mountains are ruled by the Hiisi, ancient forest gods, goblin-like creatures who dwell in forests, waters, mountains and earth. They can appear both as rock-throwing giants and very small creatures. Giant's kettles are in Finnish called Hiisi's churn (Hiidenkirnu).

The Hiisi are known for their mischievousness. They shoot arrows and push axes causing accidents and have breathed an evil spirit to snakes and iron. Still, they have preserved their status as forceful gods who are summoned in challenging situations.

O Hiisi, come from Hiitola,
Thou hump-backed from the home of gods,
Come hither with thy sons,
With thy sons and thy serving-girls,
With thy whole nation too,
With utmost speed to crush,
To eat this evil thing,
To lap this monstrous evil up.
Magic Songs of the Finns

Hiisi Queen

The Hiisi Queen or the Old Woman of Hiisi (Hiiden akka) is the female ruler of mountains, Hiisi's castles.

The Hiisi form a large household consisting of the Hiisi Queen, the Hiisi King, the girls and boys of Hiisi, the servants and the many Hiisi animals including cats, dogs, horses and ravens.

Living as a family, they do daily chores, have fun, play and sing, have weddings and parties inside the mountain and herd their own cows that rise from under the ground to pasture.

As ancient forest gods, they command bears. To protect cattle, they are asked to put burning coal under the bear's paws so that it moves faster away from the cattle and doesn't attack. In hunting spells, they put coal under hares' paws so that it runs faster toward the hunter. Hares are nicknamed Hiisi's goats.

The Hiisi have their own paths in the forest. If someone crosses their path, the person becomes so bedazzled that they can't find their way home but just keep coming back to the same spot.

They ride in a carriage wearing small bells. When you hear them approaching, it's best to throw yourself to the ground and pretend to be sleeping to make them leave you alone. They may drive away people who have made a campfire in the woods to clear the path for their wedding procession.

The Hiisi Queen is approached if someone has been lost in the forest. She is asked to open the gates to her mansion, the forest, and let the person go free.

Old wife of Hiisi,
Cheerful hostess of Hiitola,
Open your barn to me,
Open your yard,
Let go from evil distress,
From the twines of Silmutar.
Ancient Poems of the Finns

The Hiisi are masters of fire and iron and skilled blacksmiths who forge magical swords and even horses inside their doorless and windowless smithy inside the mountain. They can touch fire without burning, which is why they are called to put off fires.

Their castle is filled with weapons, protection gear and supplies like cauldrons, rags, tongs, as well as healing supplies especially for burns and bleedings. They bring kettles from their land and boil new blood in them or put their own hair in wounds to stop bleedings. During childbirth, they may take a golden axe and help with the delivery.

I'll go to seek help from a rock,
To seek strength from the stone of a hill;
In the hill there is help,
In Hiisi's castle are supplies.
Magic Songs of the Finns

The Hiisi have created many animals that travel between our world and the otherworlds: horses, elks, ravens and snakes. When snakes were born from Syöjätär's spit, the Hiisi Queen made its back of her fire poker, its eyes of her flax and its tongue of her barley.

Horses and dogs are in their command. The Hiisi Queen and King are called from the mountain to help in keeping a horse still. They control the barking of dogs by closing their mouths with locks they have forged in their smithy.

Old man of Hiisi, Hiisi's old wife,
The fiery-bearded one of hell!
Just bring some people from the hill,
From the mountain top some lumps,
To press this rascal down,
To check this violent one,
So that its foot from the swamp can't rise,
Nor its hoof from the hardened earth.
Magic Songs of the Finns

The Hiisi Queen receives suitors who come to find a bride among the Hiisi girls. She gives them tasks that are neverending, and the suitor is not meant to succeed.

The magic of the queen is preserved in her hair. When Väinämöinen made the first *kantele* (zither), he used her hair for the strings. It's a magical instrument that charms all animals of the forest.

Annukka, Hiisi Daughter

Annukka is one of the beautiful Hiisi daughters whom a blacksmith wants to marry. He travels to the Hiisi castle where the Hiisi Queen starts giving him tasks in exchange for the daughter.

First, he must plough a field of serpents with his bare hands. The second task is to catch a big salmon from a fiery river, and the third one is to run a road covered with needles and sword blades barefoot.

Every time the blacksmith returns, the Hiisi Queen has a new task for him. Upon realizing that the tasks will never stop, he gets angry and transforms himself into a smithy by turning his knee into an anvil, his shirt into bellows and his fingers into tongs.

When the Hiisi Queen asks what he is forging, he answers that he's making a knife to cut her stomach open.

In anguish, Annukka asks her mother what she should do. She tells her to take a skull of a swallow, attach feathers on it, fly up to the sky and become a star.

Annukka flies to the sky, but the blacksmith transforms himself into an eagle, flies after her and tries to eat her. Annukka changes herself into a ruffe and dives into the sea, but the blacksmith takes the form of a pike and follows her.

To escape from the water, Annukka changes herself into a seagull. That's when the blacksmith has had enough. He leaves after saying that she can stay a seagull for the rest of her life for all he cares.

Hippa, Hiisi Girl

The Hiisi are responsible for all kinds of nuisances of everyday life. Hippa, the Hiisi girl, steals milk from cows and hides it. To return it, one hides a few drops of milk at the roots of a tree and utters a spell where she's asked to bring it back.

> *O Hikitukka, Hiisi's girl,*
> *Why hast thou hid the gift of cows,*
> *To Mana conveyed my milk,*
> *My quite fresh milk to Tuonela?*
> Magic Songs of the Finns

Hippa has participated in the birth of arrows. She was washing clothes on the shore when the iron-toothed Hiisi dog brought her wood chips floating in the river, stemming from a giant, fiery oak that was cut down. She brought them to the Hiisi blacksmiths who forged them into arrows. Hippa gave strands of her hair to the blacksmiths as binding threads.

> *Hiisi's iron-toothed dog*
> *That ever runs along the shore,*
> *Chanced to be running on the beach,*

To be making the gravel rattle;
In the waves he spied the chip,
From the waves snapped out the chip
And carried it to a woman's hands,
To the finger-tips of Hiisi's girl.
Whence did he get the binding threads?
He got the binding threads
From the locks of Hiisi's girl,
From the melancholy maiden's hair.
Magic Songs of the Finns

The Hiisi girl has a cat, Kipinätär (Sparky), that can be summoned from the mountain together with the Hiisi by hitting the rock three times and asking them to rise from their coal chamber. They can be raised together with a bear.

Sparky helps catch thieves and return stolen goods. A slice of a coffin board is taken from a grave and burnt on the spot of the theft. The fire is hit with willow twigs, and the fire gods are told to go after the thief and burn them so that they can't stand still. Sparky scratches their legs until they return the stolen property.

O Hippa, one of Hiisi's daughters,
O Kipinätär, Hiisi's cat,
Tear his thighs right well,
As sparks of fire torture him,
So that he shall not sleep at night,
Shall not repose at all by day,
Without first bringing back,

Without his putting in its place
What he has ta'en,
What he has robbed,
What he has taken of my goods,
What he has got,
What he has hid.
Magic Songs of the Finns

Hiisi's cat also refers to a disease creature that witches send to scratch and bite people's toes, skin or teeth. In a spell against toothache, the cat is told to stop hacking down the teeth and ravaging the jaws.

Cease to eat, to crunch,
To fret, to gnaw, that Hiisi's cat
Cease shattering, that Lempo's dog
Cease tearing up,
Cease ravaging the jaws,
Cease hacking down the teeth!
Magic Songs of the Finns

Lempo

Lempo is a flying goddess of arrows, ravens and stinging animals. Nicknamed blue-wing, pain-wing and leather-wing, she lives in the land of the Hiisi and travels with the winds. She has feathers, wings, ears, fur and long, sharp teeth. Sometimes she's called *emälempo* (Mother Lempo).

Start skiing, Hiisi,
Start flying, Mother Lempo,
Now it's time for the Hiisi to ski,
For Mother Lempo to fly.
Ancient Poems of the Finns

Lempo is associated with the Hiisi and they often come together to push axes to cause wounds or prepare poisoned arrows in their doorless and windowless smithy. She flies around shooting arrows called Lempo's leaf-spears into people and animals, causing stinging pain.

She commands stinging and biting animals: dogs, snakes, hornets and wasps. She has contributed to the birth of snakes by forming their jaws and making their tongue of her spear. Hornets and wasps are her children, and she controls their flight by telling them when to attack and when to sting rocks and stones instead of human beings.

Arrows the devil made,
Lempo leaf-headed spears,
From the boughs of the fiery oak,
From splinters of the evil tree
In a smithy without a door,
In one quite windowless.
Magic Songs of the Finns

When seeing a wasp nest, she can be asked to put her children in chains, and if she has shot an arrow, she's asked to remove it.

Diseases that eat the flesh and bite the bone – like colic and toothache – are called Lempo's hounds. The mouth of colic is made of her jaws. Swellings on the neck are Lempo's lumps and toothaches are Lempo's dogs.

Strange swelling, Lempo's lump!
I know thine origin, from what,
Excrescence, thou wast born,
Wast bred, thou horror of the land,
Wast spun, thou Lempo's whorl,
Hast swelled up, Lempo's ball!
Magic Songs of the Finns

Ravens were created by Lempo. They are birds of deathlands that fly between the different worlds bringing diseases to the otherworld and messages of death to our world. They also carry people's sorrows away.

She made the raven with ingredients from the Hiisi land: sticks, tar, axes, pots, coal and cinder. Its breastbone was made of her spinning wheel, its tail of her sail and its guts of her needle case.

> *Well I know the raven's origin,*
> *I remember the eater's origin,*
> *From what the black bird was obtained,*
> *How the raven was bred,*
> *The scoundrelly raven, Lempo's bird,*
> *Its breastbone from Lempo's spinning-wheel,*
> *Its tail from Lempo's sail,*
> *Its shanks from crooked sticks,*
> *Its belly from a wretch's sack,*
> *Its guts from Lempo's needle-case.*
> Magic Songs of the Finns

Together with the Hiisi, she controls the barking of dogs by forging gags, locks and bars to be used when silencing watchdogs and hunting dogs. They can also put their hats and caps on the dog's nose.

> *O Hiisi, shut the dog's mouth up,*
> *Lempo, the jawbone of the dog,*
> *Fetch, Hiisi, thy tall hat,*
> *Lempo, thy broad-brimmed cap*
> *With which to stop the puppy's nose.*
> Magic Songs of the Finns

Witches use Lempo in fights against one another. She is summoned to put locks in the enemy witch's mouth to stop them from making curses or to place a bloody rug around their head so that they can't look with an evil eye. Lempo's flesh can be cut and put inside a witch's mouth or she can be sent to fly inside their mouth.

May the bloody cloak of Hiitola,
May Lempo's gory rug
Envelop thy meagre skull,
And both thine ears.
May the gag of Hiisi 'tween his teeth,
May Lempo's lock upon his jaws be forced,
May his tongue turn into stone,
May his mouth be overgrown with moss.
Magic Songs of the Finns

Lempo is linked with blood and bleedings. She can both create wounds and cure them. In the Kalevala, Lempo and Hiisi push the axe of Väinämöinen to cause a life-threatening bleeding.

In healing spells, she is asked to draw her bloody arrows from the patient's skin and fly with them over nine seas all the way to Northland and shoot them into the Iron Mountain. When cutting excess flesh off wounds, Lempo is threatened that if she pushes the knife to make it slip, she will herself be sliced with her own knife.

To make bleedings stop, the story of Lempo's family is recited: the father Lempo was cut and his head was carried to the water, the mother Lempo was cut and her head was carried to the fire, and the boy Lempo was cut and his head was brought to a swamp. Their veins were tied up and the bleeding stopped.

The idea is to prove that if the whole Lempo family could be cured from a bleeding, it should work this time too.

Father Lempo received a cut,
Into the water they flung his head;
Mother Lempo received a cut,
Into the fire they whisked her head;
Boy Lempo received a cut,
Into a swamp they stamped his head;
All the Lempos received a cut from their own knives,
Sharp knives they had made themselves,
From an instrument they made
On the top of a juniper stump,
On the end of a rolling block.
Their veins were knotted up,
So why not this vein too,
Why is the blood not stopped,
The deadly cataract not plugged?
Magic Songs of the Finns

Water

Water is the strongest realm of nature and linked with forests. It is said that the maiden of the sea and the fiancé of the forest have the same mind, the same tongue and the same heart, and their minds wander together through the wilderness and seashores.

Streams, rivers, ponds, springs and lakes have their own guardians (*haltija*) who take care of the animals and movements of waters. The gods form a large family of water goddess Vellamo, water god Ahti and the many sisters, brothers, boys and girls of the realm.

Hosts of the water,
Hostesses of the water,
Girls of the water,
Boys of the water,
Sisters of the water,
Brothers of the water,
Old men of the water,
Old women of the water,
The large family of the water,
The whole nation of the water.
Ancient Poems of the Finns

Vellamo

Vellamo is the water goddess, the Hostess of the Water (*veden emäntä*). She wears a reed dress and a foam cloak and controls the waters, waves and the fish with the water god Ahti. They protect travels by the sea by tranquillizing the waves.

> *O Ahti, tranquillise the waves,*
> *O Vellamo the water's force,*
> *Lest on the gunwale it should splash,*
> *On my bent timbers it should fall.*
> Magic Songs of the Finns

Vellamo can be asked for fishing luck by calling her through a ring. She is asked to abandon her reed dress and put on a gold and silver dress woven by the Sun goddess Päivätär and the Moon goddess Kuutar.

> *O water's mistress, Vellamo,*
> *Water's old wife with reedy breast,*
> *Come here to exchange thy shirt,*
> *To change thy clothes.*

On thee is a shirt of reeds,
On thee is a sea-foam cloak,
Made by the daughter of the wind,
The gift of Aallotar;
I give thee a linen shirt,
Of linen entirely made,
By Kuutar woven and spun by Päivätär.
Magic Songs of the Finns

If she accepts the offering and puts the dress on, it means she's willing to give fish from the sea or lake. She also assists in finding pearls. When opening clams, she's asked with songs to give a pearl.

The water gods are offered a gift from the first catch of fish in the spring. A fish is boiled and left in a kettle on the shore, and the gods are invited to eat. If no offerings are made, they are not pleased.

They also get offended if one makes noise, curses or has a fight close to the waters. If that happens, one should carve some silver to the water, otherwise their wrath will spoil the water so that it produces no more fish. If the gods get really angry, they can send out a disease.

In severe cases, a healer is required to negotiate with the gods and ask them why they got so angry that they sent their children to bite, eat, tear, break bones, twist the heart, taste the liver or eat the lungs of the patient. The healer begs for forgiveness and asks the gods to take back the disease.

Vellamo rewards those who behave respectfully toward her family. If you see her washing her hair on a rock in the water and greet her politely, she may promise to protect your family on the waters and give even more fish.

She herds her own cattle of cows under the water. A woman noticed twenty beautiful, shiny cows eating on her field and started driving them toward her barn to keep them safe for the night. But when they passed a lake, they walked one by one into it until they all disappeared. Next night, she caught a lot of fish from that lake. Another woman kept a cow of the goddess in her barn and didn't give it back until Vellamo threatened her that if she ever puts her foot in the water, she will pull her under.

Vellamo can send her own cow to people who have done favours for her. A famous flax spinner had made linen for her, and she gave her a brown, white-headed cow that had a fish tail under its belly and on its back. The spinner kept the cow for many years. It gave a lot of good milk, and only once did it try to return to the lake.

Water goddesses are often summoned for healing and protection. Vellamo can raise a whole army from the waters to protect the summoner in their fight against enemies.

> *From the water, water's mistress! Rise,*
> *Thou blue-cap from the waves,*
> *From the spring, soft-skirted one,*
> *From the mud, thou clean of face,*
> *To give strength to a strengthless man,*
> *To support an unsupported one.*
> *Raise men from the sea,*
> *Heroes from landlocked lakes,*
> *Bowmen from streams,*
> *And swordsmen from the wells.*
> *I do not want them against myself,*
> *Nor yet against my followers,*
> *I'll take them against my enemies,*
> *'Gainst the people of the enemy.*
> Magic Songs of the Finns

Girl of the Rapids

The Girl of the Rapids (*kosken tyttö*) is the guardian of rapids of streams and rivers. The churning, foamy water of rapids is the most powerful type of water. Related to storm and thunder, it's used to fight fires, especially forest fires.

It can be used in some healing rituals. Healers take mud from the bottom of a rapids, press the sore spot of the patient with it and then return it to the river. But one must be careful because of its wild nature, and a safer option is to use still water.

Rapid water is used for enhancing one's magical powers. Parents who want their child to be a magician, wash them with it before the child is three days old. The goddess raises from the water and gives some of her power to the child.

Sages who want to increase their power will go to a cliff during the first thunder of spring, take some foamy water from the river and wash their head or whole body with it while asking thunder god Ukko to strengthen their character.

The Girl of the Rapids controls the water of her realm and regulates its wildness. She protects travellers by making the water smoother to ease the passage of boats.

Sitting on a rock in the water, she spins her blue hair on a spinning wheel and makes threads that she places on the waves as paths.

Virgin of the sacred whirlpool,
Thou whose home is in the river,
Spin from flax of strongest fiber,
Spin a thread of crimson color,
Draw it gently through the water,
That the thread our ship may follow,
And our vessel pass in safety!
Kalevala

She gathers waves in her arms to still their anger and move them away from a boat's way. Those who travel by water address her in the beginning of the journey, asking her to keep the water calm. She climbs on top of the waves and hits them with a copper hammer to make them lower.

Daughter of the rapids,
Maiden of the stream,
Take your copper hammer,
With which to hit the riverbanks,
With which to lower the waves,
For me to travel the rapids,
To let me float along the stream!
Ancient Poems of the Finns

She can crush stones or turn them into moss to clear the way. Sometimes she gives an oar to the rower so they can steer the boat faster past dangers.

O gracious woman, Meletar,
Give me thy serviceable oar
With which I'll steer,
I'll shoot the spell-bound streams,
Past a jealous person's house,
Under a sorcerer's window too,
Without my pinnace sticking fast,
Without my boat receiving hurt.
Magic Songs of the Finns

In the Kalevala, the goddess is called to help when Väinämöinen's boat is travelling to Northland to negotiate with Louhi about the magic mill. She's asked to take the waves in her lap, rise on the waves to gather surges, lower the rocks on the bottom of the river and spin a thread and place it on the waves.

Gather well the foam and billows
In thine arms and still their fury,
That our ship may pass in safety!
Ye, o rocks beneath the current,
Underneath the angry waters,
Lower well your heads of danger,
Sink below our magic vessel,
That our ship may pass in safety!
Kalevala

Spring Maiden

The Maiden of the Spring (*lähteen neito*) is a goddess of healing, love and beauty who provides pure, magical water from her spring for rituals.

Spring water is powerful but also gentle and can be used in all healing, unlike water of rapids that can contain evil spirits. It can heal anything from seizures to toothache. The patient is washed at the spring, or water is taken in a bottle to a sauna for bathing.

The speciality of the Spring Maiden is recovering Lempi (love). Lempi is a fire-like, wild and capricious being commanded by those with magical powers. It can be awakened in a person so that others fall in love with them or removed so that no-one is interested in them.

If a witch has cursed a girl and hidden her Lempi, a sage is required who is specialized in reverting witches' curses and restoring love. The sage goes to a spring with the cursed girl, who is wearing a crown made of flowers, hits the water with rowan twigs and asks the Spring Maiden to rise and give permission to take water from the spring.

Rise, maiden, from the spring,
O grey-eyes from the pool,
To be a darling woman's help,
The comrade of a famous wife.
Arise and water fetch,

Some water from the spring of Love.
Pray give me water as a loan for ever,
For as long as the moon sheds a golden light.
Magic Songs of the Finns

If the maiden rises, the sage is allowed to take water. Offerings are given to the goddess by carving slices of silver into the spring from a ring or coin. The girl is washed and then walked around the spring three times while asking the goddess to make her beautiful and luxuriant in form, brighten her eyes and make her temples bloom.

Make her luxuriant in form
And beautiful of countenance,
Make bright her eyes,
Make her temples bloom,
Make nice her breasts,
Make her bosom full,
To be observed by all,
To be a wonder to herself.
Magic Songs of the Finns

After the ritual, the excess water is poured back, and silver is given to the goddess a second time to thank her. If the water is not returned to the spring, or if offerings are not made, she can get so offended that she will dry up the spring altogether and move it somewhere else.

If the ritual is successful and the girl gets married, the Spring Maiden is invited to protect her at the wedding to prevent an envious person from cursing her again. The sage performing the wedding ritual carries spring water in a small bottle to have the power of water with them.

From yonder person I ask for help,
From yonder woman I cry for aid:
From the gravel, bony-fingered,
Rise, steel-jawed, from the muddy strand,
From the spring, o maiden,
Rise, blue-socks, from a corner of the swamp.
Magic Songs of the Finns

The Spring Maiden can be called as a general helper for support in any situation to destroy the bad, conquer the enemies and crush those wishing ill.

Rise, maiden! from the spring,
From the pool, soft petticoat!
O slender fingers, from the grass,
From the withered grass,
O golden locks,
To act as my support,
To be active in my defence,
To overturn the envious,
To crush those wishing ill,
To destroy the bad,
To conquer the enemies.
Magic Songs of the Finns

Näkki

The Näkki is a water goddess of seas, lakes, rivers and wells. She can be seen sitting on a rock combing her hair with a black comb or standing in the water so that only her upper body is visible. If spoken to, she makes grimaces.

She grabs swimmers and drowns them, snatches people walking on the sea shore and pulls down those who go too near to a well. She can squeeze people to death, suck their blood or bring them to the open sea into a whirlpool. Dark spots on a drowned person's skin are suspected to be Näkki's fingerprints.

A bunch of boys were going for a swim when they saw a woman rising from the current with her hair long and wild on her shoulders and water pouring from it like streams. The other boys got scared and went home, but three boys went swimming anyway. One of them, a good swimmer, sank into the water and disappeared. The whole village tried to drag the water, but he was never found.

At times, she masks herself as an animal, running along shores in the form of a horse or a dog, and when children climb on her back, she runs into the lake. She can also appear as a black cat with long nails or a brown fox that grabs swimmers by their toes and pulls them to the deep. One can be saved by yelling her name.

Although she usually doesn't walk on dry land, she is known to sometimes sneak into houses and rob babies from their cribs. Even from afar, she can lure people to the water. A sick man had a strong feeling that he must go into the water because it was calling him day and night. He asked his family and nurse to let him go to fulfill the water's wish. When they didn't, he asked for a glass of water and drank it, but the water went down the wrong pipe, and he drowned.

If the Näkki is insulted, she takes revenge. A girl went to get water from the river and saw her sitting on the rock washing herself. When the girl told her that it's obscene, she dove into the water. The girl went to the sauna and returned to the river to wash her eyes. Next day, she was found dead at the riverside lying on her stomach and her face in the water.

It's believed that children who are tossed into the water by their mothers become a Näkki or that people whom the Näkki has drowned become a Näkki themselves.

Once, she was caught in a fishing net. The fishermen, not knowing who she was, brought her inside and offered her food, but she didn't eat anything, just sat at the stove crying that her mother and father don't know where their beloved daughter is. After three days, the men brought her back to the water, and she quickly dove in.

Precautions can be taken to avoid the Näkki. Before going swimming, throw a rock into the lake and say, "Näkki out, me in!" When coming out of the water, throw again a rock in and say, "Näkki in, me out!" One can also put a knife in the water before going swimming because she's afraid of iron.

Mermaid Aino

Aino is a young woman in the Kalevala who is sad because she has to get married to Väinämöinen. Her family members don't understand why she's unhappy, after all, he is a mighty bard and hero.

Her mother tells her she has hidden a dress and jewelry inside a chest in the shed for Aino to wear at her wedding. They are made of gold and silver by the goddesses of the Sun and the Moon.

Now make haste to yonder hill-top,
To the store-house on the mountain,
Open there the large compartment,
Thou will find it filled with boxes,
Chests and cases, trunks and boxes;
Open thou the box, the largest,
Lift away the gaudy cover,
Thou will find six golden girdles,
Seven rainbow-tinted dresses,
Woven by the Moon's fair daughters,
Fashioned by the Sun's sweet virgins.
Kalevala

Aino isn't impressed by the gold and silver but, instead, starts fantasizing about becoming a mermaid so that she could swim free in the sea as a sister of the fish. She tells her mother she should have rather told her to go into the sea under the waves than to be an old man's wife.

> Better far if thou hadst sent me
> Far below the salt-sea surges,
> To become the whiting's sister,
> And the friend of perch and salmon;
> Better far to ride the billows,
> Swim the sea-foam as a mermaid,
> And the friend of nimble fishes,
> Than to be an old man's solace.
> Kalevala

She goes to the shed, opens the chest, puts on the skirts, belts and jewelry. In great sorrow, she leaves her home and starts walking over fields and meadows, through fens and forests, singing mournful songs. After three days, she arrives at a seashore, sits down on a rock and cries all night.

Early in the morning, she glances at the sea and sees three maidens bathing in the water near a shiny, golden rock. She wants to go to that rock and become a water maiden.

> As the day dawns, looking round her,
> She beholds three water-maidens,
> On a headland jutting seaward,
> Water-maidens four in number,
> Sitting on the wave-lashed ledges,
> Swimming now upon the billows,

Now upon the rocks reposing.
Quick the weeping maiden, Aino,
Hastens there to join the mermaids,
Fairy maidens of the waters.
Kalevala

She throws away her dress and jewelry, swims to the rock and climbs on it, but it crashes down beneath her, and she falls into the sea. A hare runs to tell about her death to her mother who cries so much that her tears create three rivers. Also Väinämöinen cries for days and nights.

One day, he goes fishing and catches a fish he hasn't seen before. When he takes out a knife, the fish dives back to the water. He only realizes it's Aino when she starts scolding him for not recognizing her. Aino has become a mermaid.

I am not a scaly sea-fish,
Not a trout of Northland rivers,
Not a whiting from the waters,
Not a salmon of the North-seas,
I, a young and merry maiden,
Friend and sister of the fishes,
Youkahainen's youngest sister,
I, the one that thou dost fish for,
I am Aino whom thou lovest.
Kalevala

Earth

Gods of the earth form a large family. An older female guardian is the Matron of the Earth, an older male guardian is the Host of the Earth, and younger gods are earth's daughters, sons, girls and boys.

Earth goddesses protect the earth and soil, fields and meadows. The whole household is greeted when, for instance, bringing new cows to pasture.

> *Greetings earth,*
> *Greetings host of earth,*
> *Greetings hostess of the earth,*
> *The golden kings of the earth,*
> *The ancestors of the earth,*
> *The maidens and sons of the earth,*
> *The bought slaves of the earth,*
> *The big and small of the earth,*
> *The young and old of the earth,*
> *Give peace to the commoners,*
> *Harmony to the muddy-legs!*
> Ancient Poems of the Finns

Manutar, Earth Matron

Manutar, the Earth Matron, is the goddess of earth responsible for fertility of the soil. At the start of the sowing season, she's begged to wake up from slumber below the earth and make the grass force its way and the earth push forth straw.

> *Old wife below the ground!*
> *Earth's mistress, the soil's old wife,*
> *Cause the grass to force its way,*
> *The powerful earth to push forth shoots,*
> *Earth shows no lack of strength,*
> *Nor the grassy sward of sustenance,*
> *If the Gift-givers are inclined,*
> *If the Nature's daughters so desire.*
> Magic Songs of the Finns

Offerings are made to her at a sacrifice tree near the house. If an envious neighbor has cursed a field so that it doesn't grow grain, Manutar is asked to remove the curse and make the soil thrive again. A seed porridge is made and brought to the roots of the tree to thank her.

Houses within her realm are under her protection. When new people join the household, they are introduced to the gods and offerings are made so that they know that the person now belongs to this household.

Manutar and the other earth gods are greeted when coming home, when going to bed at night and when leaving on a journey.

She protects pastures and ensures the success of cattle on her fields. If something bad, like a fire, is about to happen, she warns the household by making an appearance to them.

To build a new house, one must find out in a dream whether the earth guardian of that spot is benevolent or not. If not, one cannot build a house there.

When moving to a new house, the gods are greeted, the house is circled with torches, and offerings like bread, salt and rye are placed in each corner while asking the gods for peace and health. .

The Earth Matron can appear to the new inhabitants at night in the form of an old woman, and her appearance reveals whether the family will have happiness. If she's dressed in fine clothes and golden earrings, the family will live happily in the new house, but if she looks sad and poor, life will be miserable.

The earth gods must be remembered continuously with offerings. Every time bread or beer is made, they are given the first tastings. For good luck with cows, they are offered milk, and when slaughtering animals, a few drops of blood are sprinkled to the ground.

Failing to make the correct offerings, making noise or leading a restless life can result in angering the house guardian. The god may leave the house altogether, which brings unfortune for a long time to come.

If Manutar is offended by something, she may show herself to the host and hostess of the house on a field wearing ragged clothes. To appease her, one takes a wedding ring and goes naked before sunrise to the spot where she was seen. Gold is carved from the ring to that spot and she is asked for forgiveness.

Manutar, hostess of the soil,
If you are awake,
Come to change our gold,
Come to change our silver,
Put your cloth on the ground,
Place your favourite linen,
So the gold doesn't go to waste,
So the silver doesn't get lost.
Ancient Poems of the Finns

Frogs, stones, snakes and insects that live inside the earth are under her rule. If a snake attacks from under the ground, she will discipline it. Stones grow in her womb, and she lulls them in a stony cradle on a wool bed. If stones have injured a person, she's summoned from the earth, asked why she let her children do harm and pleaded to put the pains back into the stone.

Manutar can be summoned to help in various situations from childbirth to fighting. To raise her, soil is taken from the ground, silver is placed down in exchange, and a summoning spell is read.

I'll raise the earth-matrons from the earth,
The mounted heroes from the sand,
To strengthen me, to give me force,
To shelter me, to give support
In this extremely toilsome work
In a time of sore distress.
Magic Songs of the Finns

Earth Maiden

Earth Maiden (*maan neito*) is a goddess who can raise an army of guardians from the ground: a hundred swordless men, a thousand men with swords. She is summoned when protection is needed in hard situations, for instance, when travelling to sorcerers' lands.

Earth's daughter! maiden of dry land,
Hark to my golden words,
Raise thy men from the earth,
From the firm dry land—thy full-grown men,
A hundred from where a stake is set,
A thousand from the corner of a stump,
A hundred swordless men,
A thousand men with swords,
To be my people, to be my strength,
To be a whole nation for me
Amid these sorcerers,
In the wizards' neighbourhood.
Magic Songs of the Finns

She gives birth to wolves by combing her hair and shaking off her head so that her hair and pearls fall to the ground.

> *There she combed her locks,*
> *She brushed her hair;*
> *She caused her pearls to chink,*
> *Her golden ornaments to clink;*
> *A pearl dropt down among the grass,*
> *Down a golden trinket crashed;*
> *From it a crafty one was born,*
> *A hairy foot was bred,*
> *A woolly tail throve well,*
> *The wolfish breed appeared.*
> Magic Songs of the Finns

If someone falls down against the earth or is startled by an earth animal, the Earth Maiden can get mad and send out her child, a disease called *maahinen* (earth elf). It's a creature with short legs that rises from the soil and attacks the person, causing eye soreness, skin rash, warts or itchiness. It's also called the secret rancour of a frog.

> *A rash (maahinen) is from the earth by birth,*
> *A red skin-spot is from the yard,*
> *From water's anger or from earth's,*
> *From the secret rancour of a frog.*
> *How it has come here now,*
> *Has come out on a human skin.*

To burn like fire, to scorch like flame,
Like a snail or like a worm,
Or like another kind of rash.
The legs of a worm are short,
An earth-elf's are shorter still.
If thou hast risen from the earth,
Then I conjure thee into earth.
Magic Songs of the Finns

To cure the *maahinen*, the healer takes a frog's head from inside the earth and presses the eye or the skin of the patient with it while reading spells that ask for forgiveness from the Earth Maiden.

Gold or silver is given to the goddess, and she is pleaded to take back her wrath, hide it in a golden cup and make the disease return to the earth.

Earth Girl, Maiden of Earth,
From the earth maahinen has risen,
To the earth return, maahinen,
Your son did bad,
Your daughter did evil,
Come to know your work,
Come to heal your bad,
Before I tell your mother.
Ancient Poems of the Finns

Osmotar

Osmotar is the goddess of beer. She created the first beer for a god's wedding, using nature's magical elements.

The brewing process is described in the origin myth and recited whenever beer is made. It works as a spell to ensure the success of the brewery.

> *The origin of ale is known,*
> *The beginning of drink is guessed:*
> *From barley is the origin of ale,*
> *Of the noble drink from hops,*
> *Yet without water it's not produced,*
> *Nor without a violent fire.*
> Magic Songs of the Finns

On the island of Päivölä, realm of the Sun, a billow of smoke is rising into the air. A big celebration is upcoming. It's a bacchanal of a secret society, the wedding of the son of the Sun.

Osmotar is responsible for making beer for the event with another nature goddess. For the whole summer, they burn wood to keep the stones heated and the water, barley and hops boiling, but the beer does not ferment.

By rubbing her palms together, Osmotar starts creating animals that will run to far-away lands and bring her ingredients.

First, she creates an iron squirrel and sends it to a forest beyond nine seas to bring back cones from a fir tree. She puts them in the caldron, but something is still missing.

She rubs her palms together again, creating a brown fox that runs to Northland and brings back honey. Still something is needed.

She creates a golden-breasted marten and sends it to the far end of Northland to a mountain cave where bears are fighting so that foam is running from their mouths. The marten takes some foam and brings it back. The beer finally starts to ferment.

> *Osmotar, the beer-preparer,*
> *Brewer of the drink refreshing,*
> *Takes the golden grains of barley,*
> *Taking six of barley-kernels,*
> *Taking seven tips of hop-fruit,*
> *Filling seven cups with water,*
> *On the fire she sets the caldron,*
> *Boils the barley, hops, and water,*
> *Lets them steep, and seethe, and bubble*
> *Brewing thus the beer delicious,*
> *In the hottest days of summer,*
> *On the foggy promontory,*
> *On the island forest-covered;*
> *Poured it into birch-wood barrels,*
> *Into hogsheads made of oak-wood.*
> *Kalevala*

In the Kalevala, Louhi hears the birth myth and makes beer for the wedding of her daughter. It's a big and happy celebration that brings truce between the rivaling realms Väinölä and Pohjola.

Now I praise the friends assembled,
All appear in graceful manners;
If the old are wise and silent,
All the youth are free and merry,
All the guests are fair and worthy.
Never was there in Wainola,
Never will there be in Northland,
Such a company assembled;
All the children speak in joyance,
All the aged move sedately;
Dressed in white are all the maidens,
Like the hoar-frost of the morning,
Like the welcome dawn of spring-time,
Like the rising of the daylight.
Silver then was more abundant,
Gold among the guests in plenty,
On the hills were money, pockets,
Money-bags along the valleys,
For the friends that were invited,
For the guests in joy assembled.
All the friends have now been lauded,
Each has gained his meed of honor.
Kalevala

Also Available on Amazon:

THE FINNISH BOOK OF THE DEAD

GODS, SPIRITS AND CREATURES OF THE UNDERWORLD
IN FINNISH MYTHOLOGY AND FOLKLORE

TIINA PORTHAN
ILLUSTRATED BY TERO PORTHAN

Afterword

We hope you enjoyed reading about mythical Finnish women of might and magic as much as we enjoyed illustrating and writing about them.

Our earlier book *The Finnish Book of the Dead: Gods, Spirits and Creatures of the Underworld in Finnish Mythology and Folklore* (2022) focuses on the gods, goddesses, animals and spirits of the underworld.

Our next book is in the process of brewing. Looking forward to seeing you on our next epic journey into Finnish poetry and ancient myths.

About the Authors

Tiina Porthan, Master of Arts, is a published author who blogs on Finnish mythology and collaborates with illustrator Tero Porthan to make Finnish mythology known worldwide.

Tero Porthan is a Finnish artist illustrating the magical world of Finnish mythology with its creatures and beings, inspired by ancient poems and songs. Tero's art has been shown in international exhibitions (Paris, Milan, Madrid) and published in several art books and magazines.

Our blog on Finnish Mythology:
https://finnmyth.wordpress.com

Tero Porthan's online galleries:
https://www.deviantart.com/teroporthan
https://www.instagram.com/teroporthan

Bibliography

Ganander, Kristfrid: *Mythologica Fennica*, Recallmed, Klaukkala, 1789

Haavio Martti: *Suomalainen mytologia*, WSOY, Porvoo, 1967

Harva Uno: Suomalaisten muinaisusko, SKS , Helsinki, 2018

Krohn Kaarle: *Suomalaisten runojen uskonto*, Salakirjat, Porvoo, 2008

Lönnrot, Elias: *The Kalevala: Finnish National Epic*, 1849, translation by John Martin Crawford, Juminkeko, Kuhmo, 2020

The Magic Songs of the Finns: sung since the time immemorial (original: *Suomen Kansan Muinaisia Loitsurunoja*). Compiled and edited by Elias Lönnrot in 1880; translated into English by John Abercromby in 1898, illustrated by Akseli Gallen-Kallela in 1922, Salakirjat, Porvoo, 2011

Porthan, Henrik Gabriel: *Suomalaisesta runoudesta*, SKS, Helsinki, 1983

Pulkkinen, Risto & Lindfors, Stina: *Suomalaisen kansanuskon sanakirja*, Gaudeamus, Helsinki, 2016

Siikala, Anna-Leena: *Suomalainen samanismi: Mielikuvien historiaa*, SKS, Helsinki, 1992

Siikala, Anna-Leena: *Itämerensuomalaisten mytologia*, SKS, Helsinki, 2012

Simonsuuri, Lauri: *Myytillisiä tarinoita*, SKS, Turenki, 2017

Suomen kansan vanhat runot, (Ancient Poems of the Finns), ancient oral tradition collected and published as a book series, 1908-1948, digital edition at skvr.fi. Translations for this book by Tiina Porthan

Made in the USA
Las Vegas, NV
28 November 2024